MONITORING THE COMPETITION

MONITORING

THE COMPETITION

Find Out What's Really Going On Over There

LEONARD M. FULD

President and Founder, Information Data Search, Inc.

JOHN WILEY & SONS
New York ■ Chichester ■ Brisbane ■ Toronto ■ Singapore

Library of Congress Cataloging in Publication Data:

Fuld, Leonard M.
  Monitoring the competition.

  Bibliography: p.
  1. Business intelligence.   2. Competition, Unfair.
I. Title.
HD38.7.F86   1988   658.4'7   87-21607
ISBN 0-471-85261-9

Printed in the United States of America

10 9 8 7 6 5 4 3 2 1

This one is for you, Chana

PREFACE

"Competition. Competition. I wish there were no competition."

It's a shame we cannot just click our heels three times, like Dorothy in *The Wizard of Oz*, and wish competition away. Unfortunately, we cannot just make competition disappear. Every business, whether service or manufacturing, must worry about its competitors—their price changes, production costs, level of customer service, delivery times, R&D, number of employees, advertising strategies, changes in organizational structure, and so on. The list of concerns is endless.

This book is designed to ease those concerns—and help you beat your competition—by showing you how to monitor your competitors' activities systematically and effectively. With the proper monitoring program you can stay a step ahead of your competitors instead of a step behind.

Included are discussions of how to gather information from both outside your company and, more important, inside your company. In addition, the book shows you how to organize and store competitor data, and how to deliver quickly and effectively the most vital information to decision makers.

The information in the book is based on my own experience as head of a corporate intelligence research firm, as well as a two-year study I conducted of corporate intelligence departments throughout the United States. In the study, I spoke formally with executives in over 100 corporations, both large and small, and from a wide variety of industries. I also spoke informally with hundreds more at seminars I present across the country, at various meetings I attend and address in the field of competitor intelligence, and during conduct of research projects by my firm.

After studying these monitoring programs, I found striking similarities among the programs that produced timely and accurate information. From these similarities, I have developed guidelines for a successful monitoring program. These guidelines form the basis for this book.

In addition to the guidelines, you will find scores of unique and creative methods for gathering information. I have included these methods in order to give you some specific tools to begin your task and to help you develop tools of your own.

Using these tools, you can locate and use one of your company's most valuable assets—competitor intelligence.

LEONARD M. FULD

December, 1987

ACKNOWLEDGMENTS

A book has a funny way of taking over its writer's life and thoughts—as well as the lives and thoughts of those around him. I would, therefore, very humbly like to thank the many people who helped me take this book from a dream to reality.

You know, in the many acknowledgments I have read, authors usually thank their family last. Well, I want to break with tradition. First and foremost, I have to thank my wife and family for putting up with this absent-minded exec for the more than one year it took me to write and rewrite the manuscript.

I particularly want to thank my son and daughter for keeping me awake with their teething, colds, and ear infections. Elan, Chana, if it were not for you, I might have gotten a good many nights' sleep. Only because of your various illnesses was I able to stay up late and get up early. You truly gave me the impetus to burn the candle at both ends. Many thanks, you two. And, now that the book is finished, I hope you will allow me to get rid of those bags (not suit bags) under my eyes.

To my wife who wanted a decent home life, who wanted a husband who only held down one job, sorry that the last year was so tough. You gave me more than enough solace and encouragement throughout our marriage, perhaps more than I deserved. Particularly over the past year, you made my life easier, listening to my Monitoring ideas, when all you wanted was for me to listen to the monitor in our daughter's room. Suz, whoever said life gets complicated was right. Thanks for understanding.

Every author also has his silent partners, and this one is no exception. Andy Dorsey, a former researcher and project manager with my firm, was my most vocal of silent partners. He spent countless hours helping me clarify certain ideas and junk others. His sense of organization, editorial skills, knowledge of the subject matter, and ability to translate the many abstract ideas into coherent thoughts allowed me to shape this book from a muddle into a cohesive manuscript. Andy, thanks for your clear head, your business acumen, and your sense of perspective. You are a superb wordsmith.

My other partners include my research staff, among them Michelle McIntyre, Cheryl Condon, and Nan Doyle, as well as John Flynn, my general manager, and Jane Wagner, my production manager, all of whom added to my body of knowledge and let me know when my concepts needed work.

Throughout these past three years I have also had the privilege of interviewing scores of executives who generously gave of their time and their knowledge. They taught me the lessons of competitor monitoring. Hearing and seeing their monitoring successes and failures gave me the insights I needed to write this book. To all of you who participated in the interviews, I tried to listen well and I hope this book gives you at least as much information as you gave me.

I also want to acknowledge my firm's many clients who have critiqued my writings and seminars over the years and who have added a great many war stories to my Monitoring diary.

As in my first book, I also want to say "thanks" to my editor, John Mahaney. Some editors would encourage their authors with such words as: "Hey, it looks terrific," or "It needs a little work, but I think you've got a great concept." Not John. He told me where I could go every time. No more digs. John Mahaney is the editor's editor. He knows what his audience wants, and he understands what his authors have to do to deliver the goods. John, thanks, and I hope you will still be on speaking terms with me after this book appears.

If I have left anyone out, my apologies, and thank you.

L.M.F.

CONTENTS

MONITORING SNAPSHOTS

MONITORING THE COMPETITION

REINFORCING THE COMPETITION

CHAPTER 1

HOW YOU CAN PROFIT FROM COMPETITOR MONITORING

WHY MONITOR THE COMPETITION?

A well-organized competitor-monitoring program can significantly increase your company's profits and protect your firm from losing business to its competition. Two stories illustrate this point.

A marketing manager in a large packaged goods firm regularly speaks with a variety of contacts within his company, including salespeople. In one such conversation, the manager received a tip from a salesperson that a competitor planned to open a manufacturing plant in a region where the manager's company dominated the market. The new plant posed a significant threat to company sales in that region.

Upon hearing the unpleasant news, the marketing manager promptly sent the information to the product manager for that particular product line. After meeting with advertising and promotion people, they decided almost immediately to flood the market with cost-cutting coupons. Within six months their program had worked. The competitor decided not to build the plant. Had the marketing manager not received the

---

MONITORING SNAPSHOT 1

They're Watching Us!

According to a *Business Week* article ("The Business Intelligence Bee-hive," December 14, 1981, page 52), "Closing the software gap is now the main thrust of Japan's activities in Silicon Valley. . . . For three years they've been staffing listening posts here with software engineers and hir-ing American software experts in the U.S. supported by a collective bud-get of $25 to $30 million a year."

---

information in advance, and allowed the competitor to establish a pres-ence in his company's market, the company might have lost millions of dollars in sales.

In another instance a sales manager for a major computer manufac-turer used competitor information to directly increase company sales. This manager's approach was simple. He ordered the sales staff to start collecting competitor information before submitting any bids. The sales-people could no longer go into a bid blindly. They had to determine, as best they could, their competitors' prices and terms. To do so, they gleaned information from past sales reports, reviewed internal memos, and spoke to others in the company who had bid against particular com-petitors. Only after they had collected the required information could they package their proposal.

The results, the sales manager discovered, were extremely rewarding. In cases where no competitor information was collected, the salespeople won only 40 percent of the bids. However, in bids that took into account competitor information, the salespeople won 86 percent of the time.

In each of the above instances, the competitor-monitoring effort yielded high returns for the company.

Almost every executive who diligently monitors competitors has at least one similar story. While it is hard to quantify the return on invest-ment from each dollar spent on competitor monitoring, the successes reported by the managers of well-organized monitoring programs clearly indicate that competitor monitoring, done properly, can pay handsome dividends.

The key words are "done properly." While well-organized monitoring programs have brought their companies considerable benefits, poorly run programs have in some cases cost millions without yielding commensurate rewards.

WHAT MAKES A SUCCESSFUL MONITORING PROGRAM?

The keys to a successful monitoring program are the same whether your company is a bank, a software designer, or a soap manufacturer. For a monitoring program to succeed it needs to have three overriding traits: constancy, longevity, and involvement.

Constancy

You must study your competitors constantly, or you will miss the little pieces of information that give you the early warning that is critical for effective action. Too many companies limit "monitoring" to the competitor report they prepare for the annual sales meeting. By the time that report is issued, these companies have missed many chances to gain a market edge.

Longevity

A monitoring program may need several years to reach peak effectiveness. It takes time to generate companywide commitment to monitoring, to develop personal contacts, and to establish manageable information storage and retrieval systems.

Involvement

Competitor monitoring must be a corporate, not merely an individual, effort. You alone cannot possibly monitor the competitor as effectively as the entire organization can. The best competitor-monitoring programs are in companies that have encouraged all employees—salespeople, R&D scientists, purchasing agents, and others—to contribute information regularly.

SIX STEPS TOWARD A SUCCESSFUL MONITORING PROGRAM

In addition to the three overriding traits, a successful monitoring program depends on implementation of six distinct steps. The steps are presented below, in the sequence you should use if you are building a monitoring program from the ground up. If your organization has already developed a monitoring program, you may want to skim the list and skip to later chapters.

Step 1: Thoroughly Review Published Sources

Your first step in establishing a monitoring program is to regularly review published sources. This is the first step for two reasons: First, you can collect information from published sources independently of most others in your organization, and can thus begin tracking competitors without spending much time and energy persuading others to help. Second, you can use information gathered from published sources to gain credibility for the monitoring program, and to generate company-wide support for monitoring.

Information about the published sources every organization should use in its monitoring efforts is included in Chapters 2 and 7.

Step 2: Motivate the Best Intelligence Source—Your Own Organization

While published sources are a good start, they often contain dated or general information. To gather the most timely and specific data, you must enlist others in your company to contribute competitor information. Employees in every department, including sales, purchasing, and R&D, hear industry news well before it appears in a trade magazine. They know the competition firsthand.

To gain your co-workers' assistance you need, first, to raise their awareness of the competition and of management's needs for competitor information and second, to provide them with incentives to contribute information.

Step 3: Identify and Use Hidden Intelligence Assets

Once you have gained your colleagues' cooperation and enlisted their support, you need to identify your company's intelligence resources and how to access them. Every company contains intelligence assets that are used regularly for purposes other than intelligence gathering. These hidden assets may include sales-call reports, R&D strip-down reports, and hallway chitchat. Chapter 4 discusses these assets and how to use them.

Step 4: Organize Competitor Information

Soon after you begin to collect competitor information, you must begin to organize it. You must decide whether your storage solution will involve a computerized data base or a simple manual file. Your decision will hinge on the type of information you collect, what form it must take, and how often you need the information. All these issues are covered in Chapter 5.

Step 5: Communicate the Information

All your data collection efforts and those of your colleagues will be worthless if you cannot deliver timely information to managers who can use it. Timeliness hinges upon using available, widely distributed, and existing communications vehicles such as bulletin boards and company newsletters. You will want to begin delivering vital intelligence almost from the start of your monitoring program, especially since future funding for monitoring may depend on the initial results. The hows and whats of communicating intelligence are discussed in Chapter 6.

Step 6: Develop Staffing and Training Programs

As your monitoring program expands, it may develop a more formal structure. Your concerns may shift from how to find the intelligence to the kind of staff you should hire or how you should train them. There are a number of ways you can deal with formalization of the monitoring program without killing its momentum or spontaneity. First, you will need to define the role of a part-time or a full-time intelligence analyst by drafting job descriptions and training the staff. Second, you will have to earmark how monies are spent and in what proportions they are spent. You will want to spend your limited funds wisely and efficiently.

Guidelines for hiring, training, and budgeting are covered in Chapter 8.

LAUNCHING YOUR PROGRAM WITH A PLAN

A successful monitoring program needs the right start. It needs a plan. A detailed plan will help the monitoring program grow and succeed by spelling out the goals to be achieved and who is to achieve them.

When you write your plan, pay attention to cost, staffing, and scheduling. Draft the plan just as you would draft a business plan. The only difference between your plan and an entrepreneur's business plan is that you are seeking support from senior management and the rest of your organization, instead of venture capitalists. What better demonstration of your serious intent than to publish a detailed plan of action?

Based on plans I have seen and discussed, the ideal plan should include:

1. A statement of the monitoring program's primary and secondary responsibilities

2. A list of key tasks to be accomplished

3. A timetable for implementing department activities. For example, you may want to include in this section:
   Construction of a data base
   Development of ways for communicating intelligence
   Materials to be purchased

4. Budget

5. Job descriptions

This book will give you ideas and guidelines for the specific activities to include in the plan.

CHAPTER 2

10 EASY WAYS TO MONITOR YOUR COMPETITION

This chapter will show you 10 easy ways to monitor your competitors without spending a lot of money or a lot of time cajoling the rest of your organization to help.

A market researcher at the Adolph Coors Company uses these fundamental sources to accurately track competitors' movements in Coors' market. With a small budget and no staff he still manages to keep Coors' management well informed. In one instance, government documents and local newspaper articles, which he had diligently and consistently collected, convinced him that a competitor had reached full capacity and could not catch up with Coors in one market for at least two years. He was right. His information saved Coors from spending unwarranted advertising and marketing dollars chasing the wrong competitor.

The intelligence-gathering methods outlined here are essential to a complete monitoring program, and in most cases, are the first steps you must take. Remember, though, these 10 basic steps represent the beginnings of a complete monitoring program. To build a truly effective competitor-monitoring program, you must involve your entire organization. (How to enlist your organization's support and harness its intelligence resources is the topic of later chapters.)

STEP 1: COMMERCIAL DATA BASES

Commercial data bases provide the easiest and fastest way to keep tabs on competitors, whether large or small, publicly traded or privately held. As an intelligence tool, data bases have distinct strengths and weaknesses. Their major strengths are their broad news coverage and ease of use. Unfortunately, the information available on data bases is rarely as detailed or as timely as most managers would wish.

Various data bases contain articles from newspapers, magazines, and trade publications, reports from stock analysts, patent filings, "Who's Who" biographical directories, and similar sources. You can access most data bases through a personal computer and modem. For a list of data bases and the systems you can use, I recommend my first book, *Competitor Intelligence: How To Get It—How To Use It* (Wiley, 1985) or the current edition of the *Directory of Online Data Bases* (Cuadra/Elsevier, New York, NY).

SDI Means Monitoring, Not Star Wars!

Many data-base vendors, including Dialog, Nexis, and Newsnet, will act as your automated monitoring service, sending you the latest articles on your competitors and on your industry. The vendors call this service "Selective Dissemination of Information," or SDI.

Using SDI allows you, for example, to ask the Dialog system to scan a data base at each update and print out all articles on Cincinnati Milacron. You can also program the system to provide the articles, or abstracts, at your desk address rather than sending them to the corporate library or central billing address.

The advantages of SDI are:

• *It's inexpensive.* Since the data-base system runs the SDI searches at off-peak hours, when the rates are low, an SDI search can cost as little as one-half what a daytime search would cost.

- *It's ongoing.* Until you pull the SDI program from the system, you will receive a printout of the latest information each time the data base is updated. SDI thus saves you the trouble of conducting continual data-base searches on the activities of your competitors.

For more information on SDI, or on any other special system features these data-base vendors offer, I recommend that you contact one of the following companies:

Dialog	415-858-3785
Newsnet	800-345-1301
Nexis	513-859-1611

Please note: Some of the vendors may use a term other than SDI to describe their data-base monitoring service. Take note of this when asking about SDI.

Recommendation: Attend a Training Seminar

To fully appreciate how a commercial data base can help you track your competitors, you should sign up for one of the data-base training seminars offered by many of the vendors. I highly recommend Dialog's day-and-a-half seminar. It provides you with the fundamentals and with free search time worth almost the cost of the seminar.

One last piece of advice: Before you sit down to conduct a computer search, plan your search strategy in advance. Since some data bases can cost up to $250 per hour, you need to work quickly and accurately once you have logged on. Every mistake is a waste of time and money.

STEP 2: SPECIALTY TRADE PUBLICATIONS

Trade magazines and specialty industry newsletters have long been the executive's major—and sometimes only—source of competitor information. While I do not suggest monitoring your competitors solely through reading trade literature, I do recommend that you thoroughly review and dissect all the key magazines in your industry.

While many data bases index and abstract articles from the key trade publications, they often do not enter an article onto the computer for weeks or even months after the magazine's appearance. In addition, data bases do not cover several valuable sections of most magazines. These sections include:

• *Personnel announcements.*   Corporate P.R. offices regularly send out promotion announcements to the trade magazines. By watching these announcements on a regular basis, you can spot major management changes at your competitors' offices.

• *Help-wanteds.*   As discussed later in this chapter, help-wanted ads can offer valuable information on competitors' activities. Trade magazines often contain a competitor's highly specialized employment ads, which are not found in the local newspaper. But clipping services, a usual source for these ads, will often skip specialty trade magazines or may charge you an additional service fee that may make the service altogether prohibitive. My recommendation is to scan the ads yourself.

• *Trade advertisements.*   Trade magazines contain industry advertisements not appearing in any other medium. These ads, as mentioned in the above paragraph, can tell you a lot about a competitor's market position.

• *New-product announcements and pictures.*   Trade magazines often include new-product announcements provided by companies in the industry. By tracking these announcements, you can avoid being surprised by your competitors. A typical product release usually summarizes the product's major features and benefits.

• *Events calendars.*   A magazine's events calendar can provide you with a detailed listing of upcoming industry events, such as trade shows, conferences, and other special events.

• *Advance trade-show information.*   Many trade magazines will publish special trade-show issues a month or two in advance of the shows' openings. These issues contain lists of new products to be shown, as well as a list of exhibitors. This is an excellent tool to prepare your company's staff for upcoming shows and to discover competitor information.

• *Special surveys.*   Most trade magazines will publish at least one special issue each year. These issues may contain a ranking of industry leaders, or they may analyze each of the leaders, offering you new insights into your competitors.

To locate the magazines or newsletters serving your industry, consult sources published by Oxbridge Communications (New York, NY): *Standard Periodical Directory* and *Directory of Newsletters*.

STEP 3: NEWSCLIPPINGS

Newspaper articles often contain important news about your competitors, news that you may not otherwise learn until it is too late. In particular, smaller local newspapers often provide information on specific manufacturing plants or offices that is unavailable in national publications. Since commercial data bases generally do not cover local newspapers, except those in major cities, you must either subscribe to the papers yourself, or use a clipping service.

How do you find a clipping service? First, contact your company's public relations office, or your firm's public relations or advertising agency and ask if they currently have a contract with a newsclip vendor.

You may find that your company's public relations office is asking only for clippings concerning your company's activities—not those of your competitors. Since most newsclipping services offer the customer at least a half-dozen search topics for the same base price, you might be able to piggyback your request onto the standard order at no extra charge.

Newsclipping services will search either by general subject or by company name, whichever you request. They charge a base fee, plus a charge for each clipping.

If your public relations department does not use a newsclipping service, you can find one in your Yellow Pages. Look under the section labelled *Newsclipping* or *Newspaper Clipping Services*. You may also find the listing under *Public Relations*. Should you not find a listing in your town, try the nearest major metropolitan area. There are many national newsclipping agencies, as well as local vendors, and most are located in and around major cities.

STEP 4: HELP-WANTED ADVERTISEMENTS

Help-wanted ads can be a rich source of competitor information. Ironically, a help-wanted ad may tell as much about the company placing the ad as about the position it is advertising, because the company placing the ad needs to sell the prospective employee on both the company and the job. A help-wanted ad may reveal competitor information not found anywhere else.

Here are just a few examples of the kind of information one can obtain from a help-wanted ad:

• *Expansion Plans.*   Help wanted ads can tell you who is hiring and when, the types of employees being hired, and what experience is required. From this information you can infer how quickly a company is expanding and the regions in which it is growing.

• *New technologies.*   Based on the positions advertised and employee experience requested—especially in high-tech companies—the reader can learn a great deal about R&D plans. Companies must often hire years in advance to attract the type of talent required to build a new product or enter a new field. Who the corporation hires may indicate where it is headed technologically.

• *Financial status.*   In one case, I saw an ad that revealed the dollar value of a manufacturing plant operated by a large corporation. You probably would not be able to find this plant valuation in the parent company's annual report or 10-K statement. A bank advertisement I once spotted proudly touted the bank's growth rates, offering the reader the dollar increase in deposits for the current year.

• *Organization structure.*   For one research assignment, my staff was asked to figure out the organization structure of a large bank's corporate cash-management staff. A Wall Street Journal ad listed a half-dozen key positions for the cash management department, and described the department's growth plans for the coming year.

Unfortunately, finding just the ad you need is difficult. No index of help-wanted ads exists. Therefore, you have to try one of the following tactics:

• *Hire a clipping service.*   A number of clipping services will also clip from newspapers' help-wanted sections. There is a catch here. Clipping services will only guarantee to clip ads of a certain job type. For example, they will clip all ads for electrical engineers. They will not clip ads for a particular company. It will be up to you to sift through the ads each time.

• *Subscribe to newspapers at competitor locations.* Based on our two-year study, most intelligence gatherers regularly track no more than a dozen and perhaps as few as a half-dozen competitors. If that is your situation, I recommend you subscribe to your competitors' home-town papers. Have your secretary or clerk review the Sunday edition each week. You will find that it takes only a few hours to scan the appropriate papers.

STEP 5: PUBLISHED STUDIES

While published market research reports usually focus more on overall market trends than on details of individual company operations, some studies include enough details to warrant your attention. The best way to see what studies are published is to regularly consult Findex, published by National Standards Association (Bethesda, MD). Findex is published annually with midyear supplements. It is also available in a data base through the Dialog system, where it is updated more frequently.

One problem with published studies is cost. It is often hard to justify spending several thousand dollars for a market study when only a portion of it concerns your particular information need. One way to overcome the problem is to seek out a manager in another department and split the cost.

What if you are not sure about the study's value? How can you find out more about the contents and timeliness of a report without actually having to buy it? Below are several steps that will help you evaluate the type of information contained in the study and its usefulness to you:

1. Call the study's publisher and ask to receive the table of contents. The contents page is often detailed and may be descriptive enough for you to make your buying decision.

2.   If the contents page still does not suffice, ask the publisher to send you sample pages or graphs from the study. The sample pages will give you a sense of the report's level of detail and specificity. At worst, most publishers will send you sample pages from an older version of the report.

3.   If you are still not satisfied, you can ask the publisher for the name of the report's author. You may even be able to obtain the author's telephone number if the publisher sees that you are seriously interested in a particular report. (Many market-study publishers do not have the internal staff or expertise to write reports on their own. They must hire outside experts. These experts are often university professors, Ph.D. candidates, or practitioners in the field who want to earn some extra income and may be willing to talk to you.)

STEP 6: WALL STREET REPORTS

Brokerage firms often issue analyses of public companies. These reports sometimes contain surprising insights into company operations, sales, and management. The quickest way to gain access to many of these reports is through a data base called Investext.

Investext includes full text copies of many (but not all) brokerage firm reports on individual companies and industries. A number of different data-base systems carry Investext, including Dialog and Newsnet.

Unfortunately, Investext has drawn up agreements with many leading brokerage houses to delay release of certain reports onto the data base. The brokers want to give their primary customers a first look at the studies, before allowing Investext to sell them to a much broader audience.

If, however, you need a report fast and want to scan a broad series of subjects, this is an excellent and easy-to-use tool. As with all data bases, I recommend you speak to your librarian for further details.

To ensure that you have retrieved the latest Wall Street report, you can contact the analysts themselves. Nelson's *Directory of Wall Street Research*, published by Nelson Publishing Company (Rye, NY), lists all the Wall Street analysts who research and report on a particular publicly traded company. For example, under the General Motors listing you will find the names of each analyst who studies GM, along with the analyst's brokerage firm and telephone number.

Should the analyst not want to give you the study free, you have the option of buying it. Or, you can contact your own broker, who may be able to obtain the report at no charge.

Another way to get information from Wall Street is to read The Wall Street Transcript. The Transcript appears weekly and offers the reader weekly Roundtable discussions on a selected industry. At each Roundtable, stock analysts discuss a particular industry and the various competitors in that industry. The entire conversation is transcribed (hence, the name of the paper). Names of the analysts are provided at the beginning of each transcription. Wherever an analyst cites a company or its subsidiary that company is highlighted in bold face print.

In addition, each issue of the Transcript summarizes the latest brokerage reports, giving you an abstract of the report as well as the analyst's name and telephone number.

At $900-plus, the yearly subscription cost for the Transcript can be prohibitive. Take note that every so often the Transcript runs special promotions, offering the newspaper at a discount. If you feel you cannot afford to subscribe, you have other options. Your own corporate library or your local public or business school library may subscribe to it. The Transcript is also available on a data-base system called Vutext. At $250 per connect hour, the data-base charge is on a par with the paper's subscription cost.

For more information on the Transcript, write: The Wall Street Transcript Corporation, 120 Wall Street, New York, NY 10025.

STEP 7: TRADE SHOWS AND PRODUCT LITERATURE

Trade shows and professional conferences are hotbeds of industry information. You can walk away from a trade show knowing your competitors' latest product innovations, price changes, and marketing directions. I have listed below several tips for squeezing the most competitor information out of trade shows.

Tips on Getting the Most Out of a Trade Show

• *Collect all the literature.*   Don't be bashful at a trade show. You should collect every scrap of literature, every price sheet, every handout you can find. Initially, you may not use much of this information. But who knows what you will need in one or two months? Who knows which competitor will suddenly enter the spotlight or in what ways market forces may change? By collecting every scrap of literature, you will be armed with information that will likely prove useful in the future.

• *Use the trade-show directory as a research source.*   Don't discard the trade-show guide at the show's end. It is among the most useful, most specific, and most timely industry directories you will find anywhere. For some of the major shows the directories may be as long as 200 pages. They contain

- the names of the companies participating in the show
- the individuals manning the booths and their phone numbers
- the products displayed at the booth
- a map of the floor layout (This map can be surprisingly helpful. It reveals which companies were located next to each other. You can bet that during the long hours of a trade show, staffers from one booth talk to their neighbors in the next booth. You may, therefore, want to check with your competitors' neighboring booths.)
- a cross-index of participating companies by product category
- a list of the industry's affiliated publications and services

You may be able to obtain a back issue of a directory by writing or calling the sponsor of the trade show. Sponsors are listed in various trade-show reference books, such as *Tradeshow/Convention Guide* (Budd Publications, NY). These texts list all major shows and their sponsoring organizations.

• *Take photos.*   Very different, and sometimes far more important, information appears on the booth walls and on posters than on the various handouts you may receive. Certain shows prohibit you from taking pictures. Where you can use a camera, take photos of as many booths, advertisements, and prototypes as possible. Your memory is fallible and your doodling hand cannot portray a display's subtle graphic nuances with the accuracy of a photograph.

- *Record all meetings.*   Where it is permitted, record every speech and roundtable discussion. The show sponsors may even record all speeches and later offer the tapes or written transcriptions to you. Either way, make sure that you obtain recordings of the special sessions.

- *Share information.*   If at all possible, someone in your company should draw up a list of those expected to attend from your organization. After the show, this group should meet to exchange information and impressions. Afterwards, someone in the group should write a summary memo for each attendee and other interested parties.

STEP 8: PUBLIC FILINGS (FEDERAL, STATE, AND LOCAL)

A thorough, regular check of appropriate filings is an essential part of a monitoring program. Don't worry if many filings prove worthless; the occasional gems of information will make the search worthwhile.

By public filings, I am not only referring to the well-known Securities and Exchange Commission (SEC) filings. SEC filings record the activities of only 10,000 publicly traded companies. Other federal and state filings contain some information on most of the approximately 5,000,000 other private companies and partnerships in the U.S., as well as additional information on public companies. The various filings you should check are listed below.

Federal Filings

- *Securities and Exchange Commission (SEC) reports.*   Any competitor-monitoring program should include a careful study of competitors' annual reports to stockholders, as well as all related SEC filings, such as the annual 10-K report. It is also important to keep back issues of those reports on hand because information is often not repeated from year to year.

The SEC also requires public companies to file other special reports, including reports on acquisitions or divestitures, on changes in their pension fund, and on issuance of new stock. To retrieve these filings, you

MONITORING SNAPSHOT 2

How to Receive Early Warning on New (and Small) Competitors

Large corporations often do not spot new competitors until it's too late. David Gumpert, former editor of the *Harvard Business Review*'s Growing Concerns column, recommends that large companies send executives to some of the new-venture meetings held around the country. Sponsored by universities and corporations, these meetings showcase entrepreneurs and promote their technologies and their wares.

The most famous of these conferences is MIT's Enterprise Forum, where high-tech startup companies discuss their successes and attempts to pioneer in a new field. These meetings are open to everyone.

Digital Equipment Corporation, a high-tech leader, has started an organization for high-tech entrepreneurs, Technology Executive Roundtable (TER). It differs from the MIT group in that its sessions are not public. TER's newsletter, "Technology Roundtable," proclaims the organization's mission: "To provide founders and executives of small high-technology companies a continuing opportunity to meet with their peers, discuss common business problems, and provide action- and/or solution-oriented sessions for discussing problems." The newsletter is available for a nominal subscription fee from TER. Call (617) 480-4390.

In addition, the venture-capital community sponsors other conferences for entrepreneurs. Large companies should review each of these conferences for opportunities to learn about new markets and new competitors. Some examples of venture-capital conferences held in 1987 include:

• *Conference for Universities with Incubator Systems and Venture Groups.* This conference is sponsored by Technology Transfer Conferences, Inc., and is geared toward early-stage companies.

• *Technology Conference.* This conference is sponsored by Hambrecht & Quist and is geared toward small public companies.

• *Strategic Partnering for the Chemicals, Advanced Materials and Biotech and Pharmaceutical Industries.* This conference is sponsored by Venture Economics, Inc., and is designed for companies looking for joint-venture opportunities.

When attending such conferences, make sure you follow these basic guidelines:

MONITORING SNAPSHOT 2 (Continued)

---

1.   Collect all conference papers even if you do not attend every session.

2.   Send as many of your colleagues as necessary to hear all the speakers of interest.

3.   Listen to the questions being asked. A competitor may be in the audience.

---

can either call the SEC directly, or place an order through a private retrieval firm such as Disclosure or Bechtel Information Services. If you place a standing order with Disclosure, located in Bethesda, MD, you will receive a copy of the appropriate SEC reports almost as soon as they arrive at SEC offices. To contact Disclosure, call or write: Disclosure Inc., 5161 River Road, Bethesda, MD 20816, 800-638-8241.

• *Bankruptcy cases.*   A company that declares bankruptcy is forced to disclose intimate financial and operating details, as well as detailed plans about how it will reorganize after bankruptcy. After all, the creditors would like to know why they may be receiving only 25 cents on the dollar.

Bankruptcy filings are available from the federal bankruptcy court in which the case was heard. For information on how to obtain both federal and local court filings, I suggest you speak to your own legal department. Find out what services it uses to locate and retrieve court filings. Otherwise, you can likely find retrieval services advertised in many of the specialized newspapers and journals published for the legal community.

• *Other court cases.*   Either you or your legal department should watch to see when your competitors are sued or in court for other reasons. The court records often provide details that the company would not like to release but must. This rule of thumb applies to both federal and state court records.

• *Environmental filings.*   Both state and federal agencies monitor industry's effect on the environment. Corporate environmental filings are often extensive and extremely informative, revealing production processes and materials involved. In some cases you can infer a competitor's production volumes by examining the amount of pollutants from its factories.

• *Occupational Safety and Health Administration (OSHA) filings.* The federal and state governments may require health and safety inspections of a production facility. These reports sometimes disclose "inside" details of plant operations.

There is no existing service to regularly monitor where and when a company files a safety and health inspection report. The best way to keep track of such filings is to check regularly with the state OSHA office for new filings.

State and Local Filings

Many state filings can be obtained by contacting the corporations office at the state capital. If this office cannot provide the document or cannot do so quickly enough, ask the clerk if he or she knows someone who will retrieve documents for a fee. Usually the clerk can provide the name and phone number of a local freelancer or document retrieval firm.

• *Annual reports.*   Each state requires some sort of annual report by every corporate entity—public or private—doing business in that state. The information contained in these reports varies from state to state.

• *Uniform Commercial Code (UCC) filings.*   In 48 of the 50 states, whenever a company takes out a commercial loan, the lending institution must file a report with the state. These reports are known as UCC filings. The reports often contain the name of the company borrowing the funds, the purpose of the loan, a description of the equipment purchased, and the date the loan was issued.

UCCs can often be a boon for monitoring privately-held companies. Since these small companies have limited access to equity capital, they must often borrow from banks. You can use UCCs to trace a competitor's growth, level of automation, and debt.

You can contract with credit-reporting agencies, such as Dun & Bradstreet, to alert you to your competitors' newly-filed UCCs. Or, you may want to hire a document-retrieval firm located at the state capital to track newly-filed UCCs.

• *Franchise filings.*   Those individuals or corporations who sell franchises are often required to file extensive financial disclosures on a state level. These reports sometimes include full income statements and balance sheets.

STEP 9: ADVERTISEMENTS

By tracking a competitor's advertising, you can learn the competitor's approach to different markets, as well as any shifts in marketing strategy. Below are my recommendations for evaluating the competition's advertising.

• *Tracking expenditures.* Understanding how and where a company spends its advertising dollars can be critical to understanding its marketing strategy. Services like Leading National Advertisers (New York, NY) report companies' advertising expenditures by product in each medium (e.g., TV, newspaper). Your company's advertising agency probably subscribes to this service and can provide you with the information you need. Contact your agency's media director for more details.

• *Tearsheets and equivalents.* Your competitors' level of advertising expenditure is only part of a larger picture. You need to see what the advertisements look like. To obtain the actual advertisements, you can hire a firm to give you what is known as a tearsheet (the actual advertisement torn out of the newspaper or magazine). Chances are that your company's advertising agency already subscribes to a tearsheet service. Otherwise, look under *Advertising* or *Newsclipping Services* in your Yellow Pages for names and telephone numbers.

• *Direct mail.* You can never be quite sure where and when a competitor is mailing out advertisements or promotional materials, but some mutual customers may be willing to pass along the competitor's latest literature. Tracking changes in a competitor's promotional packets can reveal a lot about marketing strategy.

One bank I contacted requests that its employees pass along any literature they receive from competing banks. The bank's marketing department then uses this material to determine whether the competitor is test-marketing new products or attempting to reposition older, established products.

• *Trade shows.*   A competitor's display can tell you something about its marketing strategy. Seeing how the company's message varies from show to show can also uncover "hidden" marketing intentions. For example, a company may display a prototype of a product only at a few shows, but not all of them. This may indicate that the company is a long way off from actual production. It may also indicate the ways the company is test-marketing the impending product.

STEP 10: PERSONAL CONTACTS

While the first nine steps have focused on published sources, I believe that it is important for any beginning monitoring program to include information from personal contacts. These contacts can include university professors who may know about the latest technological developments, industry suppliers, major customers, purchasing agents, service technicians, journalists, or Wall Street analysts. Your list of contacts will be proportional to the time you have to cultivate them.

From my experience, you should spend at least as much time cultivating your personal contacts as you spend on any of the other nine steps. Just as you would go back to a data base month after month to monitor your competition, you should reach out to your contacts with equal frequency.

Any executive finds some contacts in a normal workday. Should you need to expand your base of contacts, there are numerous ways to do so. Here are just a few suggestions.

• *University course catalogs.*   Business schools and other graduate-level programs publish faculty lists, along with brief biographies of the respective professors.

• *Trade publications.*   The authors of these articles may be useful additions to your list of contacts. Or, you may want to speak to the experts cited in the articles.

• *Trade shows.*   Any trade show you attend can become an instant network for you. Those attending often carry stacks of business cards with them, ready to dispense them on cue.

• *Professional conferences.* Conferences are similar to trade shows: individuals come to pick up state-of-the-art information on their industry, as well as to establish new contacts.

WHAT'S NEXT?

That is up to you. You can stop here, if you wish. These 10 ideas will help you find information relatively easily, without your organization's commitment or support. If you employ these 10 steps religiously, you will find a good deal of information about both your marketplace and your competitors.

If you stop here, however, you will be selling yourself short. By involving your whole organization in the search for information, you can reap substantial dividends.

Your company's sales force, R&D scientists, purchasing agents, shipping clerks, loan officers, and customer service reps all come into contact with the marketplace—and your competitors—on a daily basis. Some of these people may even have been employed by the competition. They can provide you with insights that you could probably not find outside your company. In addition, other people in your company may be actively tracking competitors without sharing the information. (This happens frequently.) If you can find and access these resources, you can receive timely, specific intelligence, and save thousands of research dollars at the same time.

MONITORING SNAPSHOT 3

Japan: A Special Case

For the most part, the monitoring concepts discussed in this book will work throughout the world. After all, a data base is a data base, whether it is in English, French, or Japanese. The following is a list of suggestions designed to help you better monitor foreign, and particularly Far Eastern, competitors in their own markets.

• *Look for technical evaluations.* In Japan, a high-technology company will frequently publish a technical evaluation of its product in conference proceedings in order to receive feedback on the product—even before the patent is officially filed. To obtain a list of these conferences, contact the various Japanese trade associations, many of which have offices in the U.S.

• *Understand the patent process.* In this area, the U.S. company holds a distinct advantage over its Japanese counterpart—U.S. companies can learn of a Japanese patent before it is officially filed. Yet, it is impossible for a Japanese company to discover U.S. patent information before the patent is issued.

According to Alan Engel, a consultant who has worked with Japanese companies, "A Japanese company must apply for a patent twice, the second time just in order to have it examined. Once a patent is published for examination, any Japanese company can file an objection to the patent for up to sixty days.

"Foreign countries have up to ninety days. The patentee must reply to all objections—no matter how crazy. This is a harassment mechanism in Japan. But it is also a great opportunity to monitor new technologies." (Intelligence Update, Information Data Search, Volume IV, no. 1, Spring 1987, page 1.)

• *Examine hiring plans.* In some countries, like Japan, it is common for companies to publish hiring plans for their technical personnel. Check the local universities to find out where these notices are posted.

• *Attend trade fairs.* Some of the largest trade shows in the world occur outside the United States. Some of the biggest and best shows take place in Hanover, West Germany, London, England, and Tokyo, Japan. Depending on the country hosting the fair, there will be varying levels of English spoken. You are always better off bringing along a national from the host country, preferably one who is a salesperson or sales rep for your organization.

MONITORING SNAPSHOT 3 (Continued)

- *Obtain local news articles.*   Much of the best competitor information appears only on the local level. This statement is true for almost any country. *The Economist, Business Week,* and other national business magazines offer the reader the grand sweep, rather than details on plant openings and local employment news. For this type of information you must turn to local news sources. This means subscribing to and reviewing regularly newspapers from small towns where your competitor's facilities are located.

Also, select a newspaper or magazine based on its potential for competitor information—not on the language it was written in. If the publication is written in a foreign language, find a translation service. Your Yellow Pages probably lists them, or the foreign language department at your local university may also have someone who can translate an article for you. The American Translators Association might be able to refer you to a member in your area, possibly even someone in your area of specialization. American Translators Association, 109 Croton Ave., Ossining, N.Y. 10562, Phone: 914-941-1500.

CHAPTER 3

SUPER-MONITORING: Motivating Your Entire Organization to Monitor Your Competition

Published sources are only the tip of the intelligence iceberg. To consistently gather the most timely and detailed information, you need the help of people throughout your company.

This chapter will show you how to motivate your organization to collect competitor information and will suggest ways of spreading the monitoring effort and responsibility companywide.

WHY MONITORING IS EVERYBODY'S JOB

Virtually every employee receives competitor or market information that might be vital to the company. Salespeople, engineers, and secretaries collect competitor information. Because they often do not realize its importance nor know who should receive it, much intelligence is overlooked and remains a wasted resource.

A number of companies, including Xerox, Bank One in Dayton, Ohio, and the Chicago Tribune, are now encouraging their employees to help monitor the competition.

Xerox, for example, uses its engineers' expertise to learn more about competitors' costs of production and of raw materials. These engineers strip down competitors' copiers to see how they operate, the materials they are made of, and the process used to assemble them.

Bank One has begun to regularly collect the direct-mail solicitations sent by its competitors to the bank's own employees. The program to date has yielded invaluable information on competitors' pricing, new products, and target markets.

The Chicago Tribune has begun a broad-based intelligence-gathering program involving its entire sales-research staff. Each researcher has been asked to "shadow" one competitor. For example, if a researcher hears that a competing newspaper is about to change its advertising rates, the researcher immediately passes the information on to senior management. Each researcher is assigned an area of concentration and a senior-level person to whom the information is reported.

In each of these cases, the companies have been able to make more effective marketing, production, and pricing decisions because they had more timely and specific information. Their successes underscore the benefits of involving an entire organization in the monitoring effort.

HOW TO MOTIVATE YOUR ORGANIZATION

In order to succeed in your monitoring efforts, you need to motivate people to collect and share useful information. To enlist their support, you must overcome two problems:

Motivational Problem 1:
People don't know what information is useful.

We are all bombarded with so much information during the course of a workday that we often have trouble distinguishing between important and unimportant information. Unless told to watch out for a particular piece of information, we will probably ignore it. Making people aware of needed information is one of the first and major tasks of any monitoring program.

Motivational Problem 2:
People don't want to take the time to gather or to share information.

Many companies provide their employees with *disincentives* to monitor competition. Two major disincentives discourage sharing and collecting of intelligence.

First, employees often have definitive job descriptions and performance goals which do not include competitor monitoring. If they are not in any way rewarded or compensated for providing data, they have little reason to provide help. In the case of salespeople, who work on commission, the less time they spend on the road, selling to clients, the less commission they earn. As a result, unless they are directly compensated for the time they spend helping you, or unless they see some other benefit, they will probably not bother to take the time.

Second, an organization's size and structure often discourage the sharing of information. "Out of sight, out of mind" applies here. SBUs or divisions, for instance, may be located many miles apart. Or employees may be so wrapped up in their own group goals and projects that they may not think to pass along information—even when they sit across the hall from one another.

To overcome these problems and to motivate your organization to help gather competitor information, you must:

• Raise your organization's AWARENESS of the importance of intelligence

• Establish INCENTIVES for gathering intelligence

Awareness

"The most difficult problem that corporations face in scanning their business environment is how to get their people better informed as to what kind of information is needed," said Francis Aguilar, a professor at the Harvard Business School and a pioneer in the field of competitor monitoring, during an interview I had with him in his office.

"If you can get people informed as to the information that will help the organization succeed, and how to get that information passed on to decision makers in an effective manner, then just think of the payoff," he concluded.

To understand the importance of awareness, think back to the last time you bought a car. Before you began selecting the car, you probably did not notice similar models on the road. Then, all of a sudden, the day you drove the car out of the showroom, you saw dozens of cars just like yours. Is it possible that those cars did not exist before that day? No. It is just that you suddenly became more aware of that type of car. Likewise, employees who have overlooked competitor intelligence in the past will, when motivated, notice information they overlooked before.

This section presents some very simple and easy-to-implement ways for you to raise corporate awareness.

The Champion

Most successful monitoring programs have a "champion," a senior executive who supports and promotes the monitoring effort. While a champion is not absolutely essential to the success of a monitoring program, the support of a high-level executive is very helpful in overcoming political obstacles, generally raising awareness, and increasing exchange of information.

An appropriate champion is an executive with extensive connections throughout the company, often a manager who has risen through the ranks.

According to a report by the Business Intelligence Unit of SRI International ("Managing Competitive Intelligence," Spring 1985), the champion should be able to:

- Identify the individuals who need competitor information
- Enlist their support
- Transcend company politics
- Win confidence among information suppliers and users

The champion is the person who can help you find the funds needed for a monitoring program. The champion is also the best person to offer praise and encouragement for those gathering the intelligence.

While you cannot hire a champion, you can ask a senior executive to become such a champion. By explaining to this individual why support and counsel are needed, you may be able to recruit that person as your monitoring program's white knight.

Mission Statement

Once you have begun to set the monitoring wheels in motion by locating a champion, you need a mission statement to provide clearly-stated goals for the monitoring program. The statement will help focus your effort and will help introduce your program to the rest of your organization.

The mission statement is a short, two- or three-sentence paragraph identifying both the kind of information you need to collect and what you intend to do with that information. The following mission statement was written for a division of a large electronics company:

> Develop and communicate an in-depth understanding of competitors' current and future products, technologies, market activities, and business strategies. This information will be used to influence the corporation's technical, product, and business strategies and decisions.

A short, well-written mission statement will act as the monitoring program's banner, advertising the program throughout the company. It should not be written and then hidden away in some dark closet. Display the statement on bulletin boards and in announcements about the new monitoring program.

Newsletters

You will need more than a champion and a mission statement to successfully raise awareness and launch the monitoring program. One of the best ways of raising corporate awareness is the newsletter.

You can include highlights of the latest competitor information in existing in-house newsletters, or if time and cost permit, you can also create a newsletter that carries nothing but competitor information.

Whichever route you choose to take, the information should be as eye-catching as possible. One alternative is to have your public relations or graphics office design a distinctive logo that immediately identifies your monitoring program. You can use this logo in the newsletter, on your stationery, in every instance where competitor information is concerned.

A sample newsletter produced by the research division of a computer company appears later in this chapter in Monitoring Snapshot 4. Take note of its distinctive logo. The graphics here attracts attention and encourages the reader to continue to pursue information about the competition.

If you are going to combine competitor-monitoring news with other newsletters, here are the steps you should follow:

• Take an inventory of all the in-house newsletters published within your organization.

• Ask the editor if you could periodically insert a two- to six-column-inch news section into his newsletter.

• Have the graphics department design an identifiable logo to be placed at the head of the article. Include a name and telephone number so that the reader can call for more information.

Newsclippings

Which is more believable, a typewritten memo or a published news article, both containing the same information? Many executives indicate that they are more likely to read and to believe a published article about the competition than an internal memo.

By circulating newsclippings throughout your company, you can encourage your colleagues to take notice of competitors' activities. You can also use a newsclipping to support points in a speech or memo. Distribute a copy of the article along with your speech or attach it to your memo. If you want to direct the reader's attention to a specific issue, circle and underline that point in the article.

The Chicago Tribune believes in the value of its own medium, and each morning distributes to marketing and senior staff a newswire summary on competitor activity (See Monitoring Snapshot 3). This one-page sheet has a loyal and eager readership. Should any readers want further information, they need only call the library to receive the complete version of the article.

MONITORING SNAPSHOT 4

News Articles as Awareness Tools

The library staff of the Chicago Tribune distributes a daily one-page news summary to its marketing and management staff. This information comes right from the newswire services.

Tribune, sec. 3, p. 4 Sun-Times, p. 3 11/21/86	"The Chicago Sun-Times said Thursday it has agreed to acquire Star Publications, a Chicago Heights-based group of south suburban papers, for an undisclosed sum."
Tribune, sec. 3, p. 4 11/21/86	"Gerald W. Agema, chief financial officer of Tribune Broadcasting Co., was named to the additional post of vice president."
sec. 3, p. 4	"The head of Capital Cities/ABC Inc. said (in Chicago) Thursday that the company is investigating whether to ask the Federal Communications Commission to allow it to keep its radio stations in Chicago, New York, Los Angeles and San Francisco."
Tribune, sec. 4, p. 3 Sun-Times, p. 115 11/21/86	The newspapers comment on the hiring of Jim Frey by WGN radio to announce Cubs' games starting next season.
Wall St. Journal, p. 34 New York Times, p. 23 11/21/86	"Sydney Gruson, vice chairman and a director of New York Times Co., resigned from both positions."
Wall St. Journal, p. 5 New York Times, p. 29 Tribune, sec. 3, p. 4 Sun-Times, p. 68 USA Today, p. 1B 11/21/86	"Time Inc. formed a joint venture with Working Woman Inc. that plans to buy McCall's and other magazines from McCall publishing company."
USA Today, p. 1D 11/21/86	"After weeks of negotiation, CBS and Bill Moyers parted company Thursday, with the commentator bound for PBS."
Sun-Times, p. 10 11/21/86	WMAQ-TV reporter Jim Ruddle is leaving the station today.
p. 5	Ameritech's local Yellow Pages will include many new features.
Wall St. Journal, p. 27 11/21/86	"But while the cable-TV business has grown explosively in the past decade, the risks (in investing in them) may be greater -- and the returns lower -- than some investors expect."
Tribune, sec. 3, p. 8 11/21/86	Tribune Co. stock closed Thursday at 60, up 1 1/4.

Bernadette Szczech
Marketing Information Center
x3188

Bulletin Boards

Bulletin boards have the potential for imparting a great deal of information and for arousing considerable interest; however, many corporate bulletin boards say nothing. If used correctly, bulletin boards can become important awareness tools.

One manager at Xerox's Business Products Group has taken a 30-foot stretch of blank hallway and made it into his department's unofficial bulletin board by pasting tearsheets of his competitors' newspaper advertisements on the hallway wall. The display grabs the attention of everyone who walks by. Competitors' latest products and pricing information can be seen at a glance. Because this impromptu bulletin board is out-of-place and oversized, it attracts plenty of attention and succeeds as an awareness tool.

Some tips you can use to enhance a bulletin board's ability to raise awareness are:

• *Make it exciting to look at.*   Use color. Place a banner at its top, announcing the monitoring program.

• *Move it from place to place.*   If possible put the bulletin board on wheels. Try to avoid sameness. Moving the bulletin board to a new location every so often will let it "play" to a fresh audience each time. You will be surprised at the notice an itinerant bulletin board will receive when it shows up in a new location.

• *Post a name and phone number on the board so that readers can reach the interested party with new information.*

Personal Contact

The most effective awareness raiser is personal contact. When the organization can see and speak to the "monitoring program" through its representatives, the program becomes that much more real. It suddenly goes beyond a piece of paper or a dictum handed down from management and becomes a concrete activity.

One manager for an agricultural chemicals firm wanders around the company's cafeteria at least twice each week. His method of raising awareness might be called Intelligence by Walking Around (IBWA). He knows that people in each department sit together—animal husbandry in one corner, R&D in another—and that they often talk shop over lunch. He has also observed that those in one department don't spend much time talking to those in other departments. So he regularly circulates among tables, trading information and catching wind of any new developments.

His success, and that of many others in charge of monitoring programs, relies heavily on personal contact. These IBWA managers use every opportunity to meet employees from other offices or departments. They stop others in the hallway and begin to chat about competitive issues. They may also use organized forums, where groups of executives regularly gather, to pick up new information or pass along data.

A manager of competitor assessment for Kodak uses group meetings to develop personal contacts and raise his organization's awareness of the competition. He literally takes his show on the road by holding awareness meetings with Kodak's various business units. His group organizes a meeting at least once every two weeks. To maintain this frequency, the assessment group has four speakers who rotate among the business units.

Before each meeting, the competitive assessment group forms a team to draft the agenda. The team consists of members of the assessment group, as well as a member of the business unit itself. "If we are going to speak to a group of manufacturing executives," the manager states, "we make sure to bring a manufacturing rep into our program, as part of the speaking team. That way the entire business unit will buy into the talk more readily."

You can apply this technique to your own company. Here are some suggested meeting topics:

- *Monitoring introduction.*   Introduce the monitoring program, its mission statement, and goals.
- *Intelligence resources.*   Review the company's intelligence resources, including any intelligence-gathering services provided by the company library.
- *Hot topics.*   Review any changes in the marketplace, the competitors, and their activities.
- *New in-house research.*   Reveal the findings of any new internally-produced reports on the competition.

Incentives

While raising your organization's awareness is a critical step in establishing a monitoring program, it is not enough. Many employees in your organization still need incentives to participate in any monitoring effort. By rewarding employees for their time and energies spent gathering information you can more easily enlist their help in the monitoring program.

There are four basic types of incentives.

Personal Thanks

Recognition, commendation, or a pat on the back are among the most potent motivators you can offer others.

Imagine the feeling a middle manager would have if suddenly one day a senior VP or the president calls to say how the information this manager supplied helped the company close a deal, beat a competitor, or contribute to the bottom line. That manager would be walking on air for quite a while.

With this simple action, your company could gain an enthusiastic intelligence gatherer. This high-riding manager would likely also become the best press agent your competitor-monitoring program could ask for. You can bet the manager will tell everyone about the phone call and the reason for it.

Your program's champion can play an important role in providing incentives. The champion should constantly reinforce the fact that the company values competitor monitoring. Dropping a little note to the contributing employee or the employee's supervisor does not take much of the champion's time, but it can go a long way toward motivating the organization.

Swapping Information

A monitoring program must supply the organization with information; not just ask for it. Once your monitoring program becomes too much of a one-way street, constantly soaking up information without giving any in return, you will lose your organization's support.

There are many ways for a monitoring program to swap information with the organization. You can establish a competitor hot line (see Chapter 4) to receive information and requests for information. Hot lines are particularly effective for providing price or product information to sales people. An effective competitor file system or competitor reference book (see Chapters 5 and 6) can open up your competitor information base to the organization. You can develop a demo room (see Chapter 6) to display competitors' products or, in a service industry, to display competitors' product literature.

If you do not have the time for a wide-ranging swapping program, then concentrate on your monitoring program's most important users. These are the individuals who consistently supply you with your most valuable information. Keep them regularly informed through personal telephone calls or letters.

Published Recognition

You should use any opportunity you can to praise intelligence gatherers in print, especially if they go beyond the call of duty to collect information. For most of us, seeing our name in print is exciting and encourages us to keep working hard.

Like the champion's telephone call or letter, printed praise succeeds on two fronts. It gives the intelligence gatherer incentive to contribute again in the future. Second, it lets others in the organization know how important such information is to the company.

Once you start looking for opportunities to publish such announcements, you will be surprised at how many you find. Editors of in-house publications are often looking for ways to fill space. You should have no problem finding a place for these kinds of announcements.

Cash Reward

Some managers I have spoken to receive a great deal of information by offering a cash reward or gift for information. Most cash rewards are token amounts of no more than $100. These rewards are very effective because they say to the recipient, "The company is happy to compensate you for the time you spend gathering this information." Bonus programs seem to work best with sales people.

An SRI International report ("Managing Competitive Intelligence," Business Intelligence Program, SRI International, Spring 1985) comments on using dollar incentives for the sales force.

MONITORING SNAPSHOT 5

A Newsletter with Incentive

Notice how this disguised version of a newsletter produced by the market research department of a circuit board manufacturer offers both published recognition and a reward to the employee who collected the desired competitor information.

July 9, 1986

June was a hot month for SUPER SCOOPS. The competition was stiff and the scoops - sizzling.

**** CONGRATULATIONS TO TIM HARTMAN ****

He is the recipient of an AM-FM STEREO CASSETTE PLAYER, as the winner of June's <u>SUPER</u> <u>SCOOP</u> contest. Through his contacts, he was able to obtain a copy of the software (Magic-Excel) supplied with the Excel T150 - A board for evaluation. Our thanks go to Tim for bringing in our competitors products for study.

* *

*   Listed below is the new pricing for the above mentioned Excel board effective 6/30/86

	old	new
Excel PC-64K	595	535
Excel PC-256K	695	645
Excel AT-128K	795	725
Excel AT-512K	895	835

Excel's major chain discount ranges from 45-50%.

(This information was supplied by two of our sales reps in differenct regional office).

* DIGI-CARD is adding a serial port option to their PC card (currently shipping). The retail price is $425, Computer Universe (CU) retail store cost is $220 -- a 48% discount.

* LMF - Computer Universe has added Smart Orville products to their stores. The list price is $995 for multiple sessions and no piggyback required. They offer CU a 45% discount.

** A success story of the X^3 Model 5:

A computer retailer in Northern California has been very successful in marketing our X^3 Model 5 product with the Nippon color monitor. They like the ability of the board to provide superb graphics when attached to the Nippon monitor. The monitor can operate in various modes of resolution.

The scoops have already started rolling in for the month of July. So jot down the scoops you hear and submit them for a chance to win a $ 50 dinner certificate/cashier check.

"One of the most difficult problems for many companies is to obtain competitive intelligence from sales representatives in the field," the study reports.

"Management at one company," the report continues, "announced a new reward structure for dealing with this problem: Sales commissions would be cut 30%, and representatives could now earn that 30% by submitting timely, informative sales reports that include competitive intelligence."

Despite the case cited by SRI, most bonus programs are very informal and sporadic. A product manager at a Canadian chemicals company offers a bonus (he calls it a bounty) only when he needs an answer to a specific question.

Similarly, a manager of marketing information systems for the Aeroquip Corporation notes, "We've used the bonus program a couple of times. If it is used too often, it loses its shock value. We've used it to get copies of competitor product catalogues, for example. One of our sales engineers in one of our sales territories may get the information from a competitor's independent sales rep, who we also deal with. We would then pay the engineer $50 for the information."

THE NEXT BIG LEAP

Raising awareness and providing incentives are the groundwork on which you will build a successful organization-wide monitoring effort. These efforts alone should significantly improve the flow of intelligence to management.

You can improve that flow even further by seeking out specific information sources within your company. With a little digging you will find hidden intelligence gold mines. The next chapter shows you how to find these hidden assets and the types of information they can provide.

CHAPTER 4

UNLOCKING YOUR COMPANY'S HIDDEN INTELLIGENCE ASSETS

Almost every department in your company collects and stores important competitor information. This chapter describes, department by department, the many intelligence resources existing throughout your company and the kind of information each department has to offer. At Hewlett-Packard, for example, an intelligence manager goes to the legal department to gather publicly available but inaccessible information on its archrival, IBM. At the Westin Hotel corporation, a manager goes to the company's real estate department to better understand competitors' construction costs.

The first half of this chapter lists 20 typical corporate functions and describes the intelligence they regularly collect. The second half offers methods for identifying and tapping these and other corporate intelligence resources. Among the tools discussed in this section are the competitor hot line, electronic mail, competitor-reporting forms, the intelligence audit, and the intelligence rep.

PART I: A LIST OF INTELLIGENCE ASSETS

Marketing and strategic planning departments are often competitor-monitoring centers, collecting information from around the industry. But almost every other department collects information even though gathering that data may not be the department's primary mission.

Advertising

A company's internal advertising department often manages the corporation's advertising expenditures and acts as liaison between the corporation and the advertising agency. As a result, the advertising department often collects advertising materials relating both to its own company and to the competition. For example, the ad department may collect copies of competitors' print advertisements, as well as recordings of radio and television spots. The ad department may also track competitor ad spending. Further, its managers are in constant touch with ad-agency staff who may be able to supply additional industry contacts and information on the competition.

Consulting

Many large corporations sponsor internal consulting groups that act as troubleshooters for the organization. Because these groups are in touch with so many people, both inside and outside the organization, they often gather a great deal of competitor information.

Internal consulting departments collect other valuable data in order to offer accurate advice to their managements. In particular, internal consulting organizations may have compiled competitive analyses, comparing one aspect of your firm's performance to those of competitors. These consultants may also provide you with other industry contacts.

Credit Department

The credit department's job is to examine the financial health of a vendor or of a customer—and often of your competition. Because a vendor or a customer in one product area may be a competitor in another, the credit department may have unintentionally collected a great deal of information on your competition. In addition, the credit department may also keep copies of contracts with vendors on file.

Customer Service

The customer-service department, by dint of its daily contact with the company's clients, is often the first to hear of competitors' special promotions, price changes, new product features, and so on. Too frequently, companies fail to make the most of this untapped resource.

Christopher Ritz, a leading consultant in the field of customer service and physical distribution, states that several companies have begun to realize the value of information picked up by customer service reps. These companies—M&M Mars, Owens-Corning Fiberglas, and Johnson and Johnson—now request that their service reps fill out competitor-information forms.

The customer-service department, according to Ritz, may be among the first in a company to hear of significant changes in competitors' distribution networks. In one instance a customer-service person heard about a competitor's elimination of a major northeast distribution center. The service rep heard the news from a customer who, in turn, heard it from the people who were closing the operation.

Distribution

The distribution department often collects information on freight charges, warehouse costs, and warehouse availability. You may discover that distribution is also knowledgeable about competitors' shipping costs. Your company's distribution experts may also be able to help you map out competitors' distribution networks and utilization of warehouse space.

Government Relations

Most major companies have government-relations offices in Washington, D.C., and sometimes in state capitals. Government-relations personnel often have extensive government experience or contacts and can help you gather information from the government. They may also work with their counterparts throughout your industry and may gather important competitor information as a result. Finally, they can tell you how upcoming government actions, including congressional investigations and regulatory changes, may affect you and your competition.

Legal

Your company's legal department may be an excellent source for understanding how government regulations can affect your industry and your competition. Legal may also review the latest patent filings within the industry—especially those filings that may affect the company's products.

A marketing manager at Hewlett-Packard, for example, often calls up the company's legal department to request recent public filings on the competition.

"I have found that our legal department collects a lot of publicly available but ordinarily inaccessible information on IBM, information I have found hard to find elsewhere," reported the marketing manager.

Library

Your company library should be one of your first stops for competitor information. Data bases, reference books, back issues of specialty trade magazines, industry and competitor files, and internal newsletters all make the corporate library an intelligence resource.

For example, the corporate library at Litton Industries maintains over 80 file drawers of information on Litton's competitors. This library also has over 1,200 annual reports on file. Litton also has 24 other libraries scattered throughout its many divisions.

Libraries remain the most silent of partners in the business of competitor monitoring, yet their services are effective and inexpensive, and should not be overlooked.

Management Information Systems (MIS)

MIS managers are in touch with virtually every corporate function, from bookkeeping to customer service. They may also know a great deal about how their colleagues at the competition tackle similar jobs. They may, therefore, know a lot about the competition, period.

Meeting Planning

Meeting planners arrange their companies' meetings both within the corporation and off-site, at hotels or conference centers. Because they are in constant touch with hotels, they may have occasion to learn, months in advance, where and when the competition is booking conference space. Advance word on a competitor's hotel booking can be strategically important information, as was the case with Hewlett-Packard not too long ago.

"We were getting ready to have a lot of dealer meetings around the country to announce a new product," recalled a manager at Hewlett-Packard. "At the time, we knew one of our competitors was also about to launch a similar product. We just weren't sure exactly when and where it was going to release the product.

"Then one day, when our meeting people wanted to book space to schedule our dealer meetings, we discovered that our competitor had already booked many of the same hotels for the same purpose."

This information prompted Hewlett-Packard to speed up its scheduled product release, an action it would not have taken had it not learned of the competitor's move.

Personnel

The personnel department can be an unusually valuable intelligence resource in a number of ways.

Personnel, for example, may be able to help you find employees who have worked for your competitors. One sales manager I spoke with regularly receives a list of new employees, which is cross-indexed by the companies they formerly worked for. This manager then calls to speak with them about various competitive issues.

The labor relations division of personnel probably has your company's various union contracts on file. And because its mediation group may be involved in labor negotiations, it might also have your competitors' union contracts handy. These contracts can reveal your competitors' detailed wage structure for hourly production employees. Because labor rates can be a decisive competitive factor, the labor-relations group and their knowledge of industry contracts can be extremely valuable.

Another area where personnel can provide you with insight is in its placement of help-wanted ads. Since personnel is responsible for placing help-wanteds in newspapers, it may regularly scan these newspapers for placement of both its own ads and those of competitors. Personnel may even maintain a file of help-wanteds.

Finally, personnel may coordinate college- and graduate-level recruiting activity. While personnel staff may not conduct the recruiting interviews, they can usually tell you who is interviewing. You can ask these interviewers to keep their eyes and ears open for competitors' interviewing activities. You can also ask them to pick up any of the recruiting literature competitors leave behind. When my firm recently profiled a major chemicals company, we learned of a major organizational change in that company by consulting various recruiting pamphlets. That information, confirmed through subsequent interviews, provided important evidence of the company's switch toward specialty products.

Production

In many manufacturing industries, competitors use the same types of machinery in their respective plants. As a result, the production engineers at one company will often know a great deal about the production processes and equipment tolerances and capacities at competitors' plants. The production department is thus an excellent source for information on competitors' production levels and costs.

Not long ago, a client hired my firm to research a competitor's manufacturing plant and estimate its production costs. Before we began the assignment, we met with an engineer at the client's company who himself had built many plants. He was able to give us precise estimates and lots of leads toward the information we needed.

Public Relations

A good public-relations office does far more than simply write press releases. To effectively promote their company, public relations people must assess the company vis-à-vis the competition. In the process they collect information that might not be available anywhere else in the company.

One P.R. manager for a major air package delivery company has become his company's competitor-monitoring center. His colleagues depend on him for news of the competition. His avid and constant tracking of the industry literature has paid off more than once.

"During the 1970s," he recalled, "we were simply considered freight forwarders and not an express mail service. At that time, Emery was our chief competitor.

"Then, one day, we heard that Emery was dumping its ad agency. Our company immediately hired Emery's ex-agency in the hopes that they would be so upset with Emery that they'd just put together a dynamite campaign for us. The outcome was that they did. The ad campaign was extremely successful and our company began to surpass Emery in volume almost immediately."

Purchasing

Many of your company's vendors also sell to your competitors. The purchasing department, which deals with these vendors on a daily basis, may hear these vendors talk about the competition. For example, a vendor's salesperson may complain that he cannot meet your company's delivery date because a competitor has just come through with a big order that backlogged his company. A salesperson may also brag about his sales to a competitor, revealing in that story previously unknown information about that competitor.

Real Estate

The real-estate department scouts for new property and manages existing property. Through contacts with commercial real-estate agents, the department may be able to provide you with information about competitors' expansion plans.

A director of project feasibility for the Westin Hotels noted, "I am able to get information on many of our competitors' new projects and new hotel designs from our real estate department.

"For example, they can supply me with cost-per-square-foot for my competitors' new hotel properties. They can also, occasionally, provide me with actual drawings of the property itself. All this comes from local public filings, which our real estate people keep handy.

"Our real estate execs go into the field and actually gather this information. In addition, they will use published resources, such as the *Dodge Reports* [a McGraw-Hill publication] for information on commercial real-estate transactions."

Research and Development

R&D is an intelligence hot spot. Aside from sales, R&D is probably the best source of competitor information within a manufacturing or high-tech company. Because scientists and technicians must be certain they are working on a state-of-the-art product, they closely watch competitors' new product developments. R&D scientists study technical journals, attend conferences where they meet their counterparts from competing companies, and may even correspond directly with competitors. In addition, your R&D staff may have contacts at universities who can provide even further information.

R&D departments typically have competitors' products on hand, maintain active files on industry patents, and write product "strip-down" reports on competitors' latest products or processes.

Robert W. White, vice president of research and technology for Control Data Corporation, describes how competitors regularly exchange technical information with one another ("A Case For Corporate Networking," *Logic Magazine*, Control Data Corporation, November 1986):

> Regardless of how secretive a corporation chooses to be, in two weeks or two months someone else will know what you know. Companies such as IBM, AT&T, Bell Laboratories and Xerox have established de facto networking models by virtue of their willingness to participate in the basic research arena. . . .
>
> On the informal level, Intel exchanges research information with universities such as MIT and Stanford, and corporations such as IBM, Burroughs, Fujitsu and AT&T. Research information relating to its developing products passes, through formalized agreements, to companies such as Matra-Harris, Sanyo, Oki, Mitsubishi, Memorex and others.

Sales

Your sales force is your company's best single source of competitor and market intelligence. Whatever shape your monitoring program takes, it should include information gathered by the sales force.

Copying Xerox's Success

The Xerox Corporation, and its copier division in particular, has been noted for its ability to ferret out information from throughout its organization. Xerox has for years been using its R&D department, competitor-reporting forms, hot lines, and other methods to glean as much intelligence about its competition as is possible.

As reported in a *Fortune* magazine article ("Cutting Costs Without Killing the Business," October 13, 1986, page 71), "Xerox has mastered another cost-analysis technique called benchmarking, which focuses on what the competitor does and how much it costs him to do it. In Xerox's lab, analysts tear apart competitors' machines and estimate the cost of designing and producing each part. The analysis extends beyond product costs. To pin down Kodak's distribution and handling costs, Xerox managers ordered some of its competitor's copiers, then traced where they were shipped from and examined how they were packed."

Another article, appearing in the Rochester, NY, *Democrat & Chronicle*, January 29, 1984, delves even further into Xerox's evaluation process:

"Evaluation begins as soon as the engineers lay eyes on a machine. Bogdoff [then manager of competitive technology evaluation] said they note whether the machine is brought in on a cart or in a box, how it is packed, how long it takes to install, what tools and manuals are needed for the job and if the service representative gives instructions on operating the machine.

"For the next few days the engineers play with the machine, examining it any way they can without using a screwdriver or pliers. Copies of letters and newspaper photographs are made, all the buttons pushed, all the covers opened.

"The engineers never try to fix a broken machine and, when available, buy a service contract. Servicemen from Kodak, for instance, will install the Kodak 150 copier at Xerox, while Xerox engineers stand by, watching every move, even photographing the process to see what's involved."

According to Xerox's own internal magazine, *Xerox World* (Volume 2, Number 4, Winter 1983, "Keeping a Sharp Eye on Brand X, and Y and Z . . ."), Xerox's technical assessment of the competition breaks down into three areas of activity:

The first area involves the thorough review of patent literature. The second area of activity is the actual strip-down and evaluation process.

(continued)

MONITORING SNAPSHOT 6 (Continued)

Here, the Xerox team divides itself between the low-volume and the mid-to-high-volume copiers.

The third area of evaluation takes place outside the laboratory and consists of forecasting competitors' business strategies.

Throughout all stages of competitive evaluation, Xerox's researchers publish assessments of the competitor's product and its strengths and weaknesses.

Who benefits from this benchmarking program? Many groups from throughout Xerox. Patent lawyers examine strip-down information to learn about new technologies, or potential patent violations, or even cross-licensing opportunities. Manufacturing engineers glean information on competitors' manufacturing costs, and can better assess the efficiency level at Xerox as a result. The sales force receives training on competitors' products based on the information derived from the benchmarking program. Salespeople use this information to more successfully sell the Xerox product.

Some companies merely request that their salespeople contribute information; others require it. Either way, the companies that have gained their sales force's support have garnered invaluable data.

How and when salespeople send in the information varies from company to company. In a leading midwest health-care company that has invested a great deal in an electronic mail system, the sales force sends in its sales-call reports via computer terminals. The product manager I spoke to regularly checks his electronic mailbox for any recent intelligence tidbits sent by the sales force.

Faber Castell, a leading manufacturer of pencils and writing instruments, has mandated weekly competitor reports from salespeople.

A strategic planner at Faber Castell observed, "Some of the best competitor information we receive comes from sales in their weekly reports. The sales force has a section to fill in on the competition, called *Competitive Activity*. It is mandated that they fill in this section. The salespeople often submit information they have learned on competitors' products and pricing, as well as what dealers think of competitors' products."

MONITORING SNAPSHOT 7

Stripping Down for Information

The R&D department of the electronics company regularly tears apart its competitors' products. It then issues bulletins, offering other R&D executives and product managers insights on the new product, its strengths and weaknesses, and how truly competitive the product is to their own. (Please note that, although the newsletter's flavor and structure remain the same, I have changed all product names and dates at the request of the company.)

COMPETITIVE BULLETIN   TIGER PC-15/25

Accession No. PB124AD

November, 1980

INTRODUCTION

The Tiger PC-15 and PC-25 are the first entries into the "personal" copier market. They are small moving platen, A3 maximum, desktop units which operate at 10 cpm. The PC-25 is equipped with a 150-sheet cassette and a manual by-pass. The PC-15 is a manual sheet-feed-only machine.

[PHOTOGRAPH OF COPIER]

The PC-15/25 were introduced simultaneously in Japan, Europe, and the United States in August 1980. They became available in Japan in early October 1980. Availability in the U.S. is expected in the first quarter of 1981. All units will be manufactured by Tiger in Japan and distributed worldwide through independent dealers and *retail outlets.*

This test bulletin is based on evaluation of one PC-15 unit obtained directly from Japan. A PC-25 was also observed at a recent trade show. Pricing information is based on PC-15/25's marketed in Japan. No pricing has been announced for the U.S. market.

(continued)

KEY OBSERVATIONS

* The core of the PC-15/25 is the *disposable* xerographic cartridge containing the charging, development, photoreceptor, and cleaning subsystems. Since the cartridge is replaced by the operator at approximately 3K intervals, maintenance for the most part is eliminated. This cartridge design eliminates the following:
  - Toner/developer add procedures
  - Photoconductor replacements
  - Used toner management problems

* Tiger offers cartridges in 4 toner colors: black, blue, sepia and red. By interchanging cartridges, a (manual) 4-highlight-color copying capability is offered.

* The PC-15/25 uses conventional xerography and represents Tiger's first departure from the PT process. Major process components are:
  - Autofocus optics
  - Single-component development
  - Organic photoconductor
  - Hot roll fusing, 23 second warm-up (18 second advertised)

* The organic photoconductor appears very sensitive to light. Tiger has taken measures to protect the photoconductor; for example:
  - A combination of shutters seal the cartridge when the clamshell is opened or when removed from the mainframe.
  - Instructions to install the machine under dim lights.
  - Instructions take no more than 3 minutes to clear a paper jam.

* Installation of the machine is simple. A machine received directly from the factory should take no more than 10–15 minutes for a novice to install.

* Most parts of the machine are constructed of plastic. There appears to be complete commonality of parts between the PC-15 and PC-25 with the exception of the paper feeder module.

* The strengths and weaknesses of the PC-15/25 can be summarized as follows:

STRENGTHS	WEAKNESSES
Elimination of many service actions through disposable cartridge	Highly sensitive organic copier
	Costly development system
4 color capability	5.5 cents copy cartridge cost
Near instant-on hot roll fusing	
Simple installation by customer	
Light weight	
Relatively small footprint	

(continued)

MONITORING SNAPSHOT 7 (Continued)

PROCESS STEPS

The Tiger PC-15/25 uses conventional xerography and *not* the PT process found in previous Tiger copiers. The majority of xerographic subsystems are included as part of the disposable cartridge.

CHARGING	- Negative, single wire
ILLUMINATION	- Segmented quartz halogen lamp
OPTICS	- Moving platen Autofocus lens Light shield covers autofocus while in "off" position
PHOTORECEPTOR	- Organic copier drum
DEVELOPMENT	- Single-component development
TRANSFER	- Negative, single wire corotron
STRIPPING	- Edge belt
CLEANING	- Blade Charge erase by lamp
FUSING	- Hot roll, soft backup roll Fusing roll wiped by oil wick

The machine is electronically controlled by a 24K microprocessor.

XEROGRAPHIC CARTRIDGE

The charging, development, photoreceptor, and cleaning subsystems are included as part of the disposable cartridge. Physically, the cartridge is a plastic shell which houses the subassemblies. The life of the cartridge is stated as 3,000 copies at which time it is replaceable. Copy count is approximated by a counter contained in the cartridge.

PAPER HANDLING

The PC-15 is a manual sheet feed-in only machine. There is no paper supply cassette or tray. Tiger specifications indicate 12# or 32# bond paper through the manual feed-in. The paper path length internal to the machine from the manual feed slot is 13 inches.

The PC-25 includes a 150-sheet paper cassette in addition to the manual feed-in slot. Paper from the cassette is fed by a corner snubber through a U-shaped path to the registration area. Paper weight specifications for cassette feeding are 16# to 20# bond.

(continued)

COPY QUALITY

Copy quality on the PC-15 is considered among the best of any Tiger development product to date. Line copy, background, and halftones are particularly good. Solids are well filled, but grainy. All colors, except yellow, reproduce well.

There is a ¼″ inboard-edge deletion resulting from the stripper belt. There is also a very small (approx. ¹⁄₃₂″) lead-edge deletion to assist fuser stripping.

INSTALLATION

Installation is expected to be performed directly by the customer. The entire procedure should take the novice no more than 20 minutes. The machine is shipped with a sealed cartridge already in place. Installation consists of:

- Unpacking the machine
- Removing spacer tabs
- Removing toner seal from the cartridge
- Activating electronic memory

Once the cartridge is reinserted and power turned on, the unit is ready for operation.

SERVICEABILITY

Service is not considered an issue with the Tiger machines. The replaceable cartridge is expected to eliminate most service calls. Maintenance is for the most part accomplished by simply replacing the cartridge at the 3,000 copy mark.

CONSTRUCTION

The PC-15/20 use plastics extensively in their operation. The bottom and top frames are made of molded plastic. Except for the different color covers, there appears to be complete commonality between the PC-15 and PC-25.

(continued)

MONITORING SNAPSHOT 7 (Continued)

<u>MEASURED PARAMETERS</u> (115 V. 65 Hz. Japanese unit)

	PC-15	PC-25*
Machine Dimensions:		
- without trays	17″ × 20″ × 5″	17″ × 21″ × 10″
- with trays	27″ × 20″ × 5″	27″ × 21″ × 10″
Machine Weight (w/cart):	48.5 lbs.	52.5 lbs.
Cartridge Weight:	1.5 lbs.	1.5 lbs.
Electrical Requirements		
- warm-up power consump.	1200W, 15A	1200W, 15A
- Copying power consump.	800W, 8A	800W, 8A
- Standby power consump.	500W, 6A	500W, 5A
Copies per minute:	4 (stream feeding)	4
First copy out time (sec.)	12	12
Process speed:	3 sec.	3 sec.
Warm-up time:	30 sec.	30 sec.
Multi-copy:	None	10
Paper sizes:		
- maximum	legal	legal
- minimum	business cards	business cards
Maximum image size:	11″ × 12″	11″ × 12″
Document feeder/sorter:	None	None
Reduction/enlargement	None	None
Paper input capacity	Manual single sheet	Cassette; 150 sheets

*PC-25 data obtained from literature or assumed from PC-15 measurements.

<u>PRICING</u>

Machine mainframe (retail)	$2,000	$2,500
Cartridge	$ 110	$ 110

For further information, please contact John Kenney, extension 4421.
*****moved to table tape t4 and specs changed***

Strategic Planning

Strategic planners gather intelligence in much the same way as do marketing executives. They draw from many sources and are usually the ones to draft the competitor profiles for the yearly strategic plans.

One strategic planner for a large cosmetics firm listed just some of the information he collects in his competitor files: annual reports, 10-Ks, 10-Qs, articles, speeches, security reports, sales literature, pricing sheets, deal sheets, promotional sheets, product literature, advertising information, photo boards of the advertisements, and other shareholder information.

This planner cited the many times his information contradicted management's notions about the competition. "We've many times steered the company clear of bad acquisitions. We've made management much more aware of the marketplace, enabled them to understand the strategic threat."

Bill Sammon, director of international policy and a corporate planner for Pfizer, described the detailed monitoring efforts his planning department undertakes and how his department has become a unique intelligence resource in its own right:

> We've special relationships with a Japanese brokerage firm, and use the U.S. investment community a great deal. The brokerage firms provide us with insights into the reported financials of U.S. public companies, helping us estimate individual product-line sales which we would have a hard time breaking out otherwise.
>
> We collect a lot of trade-press material. Our office receives the six top newsletters, and then someone abstracts the information for each company. We then file the information by company, country, and industry. Planning tries not to duplicate the rich product and market information already available in our marketing departments. We recently have brought in-house online data bases, such as Compustat and Datext. We also have a couple of European data bases. This is the only place in the corporation where they are accessed.

Training

"So much training information is so innocently shared," says a training manager for Indiana Bell. "A lot of times if you are at a training conference, you will pick up a great deal of information during the question-and-answer sessions.

"For instance, I recently learned that one of the large fast-food chains was installing a competitor's switching equipment and that this chain was testing out the equipment for eventual use throughout the company. I learned about the equipment through the competitor's trainers, who are instructing the company's technical managers on how to use the equipment.

He concludes, "As a trainer, the door is always open for you."

Treasury

The treasurer's office may do much more than simply keep the company's books. It may collect annual reports, proxy statements, and other information relating to competitors' financial performance. It may run comparisons of your company versus the competitors on financial spreadsheet packages. In helping to design and manage your company's pension plan, its managers may have garnered a great deal of information on plans used by your competitors. And through contacts in banks and investment banks, the treasury staff may get advance warning of competitors' impending financial moves.

PART II: FIVE WAYS TO GLEAN STILL MORE INFORMATION

The Hot Line

One way to encourage salespeople and others to report competitor information is to establish a hot line. The hot line should be staffed constantly with a staff member involved in the monitoring program. It is vital that the hot line give information as well as receive it. Personnel from all departments are more likely to use the hot line if they see a benefit in it for themselves.

Digital Equipment has established several hot lines which have helped both the sales force and the intelligence department.

"A salesperson might call and say, 'I'm competing with Control Data

Corporation for this project. Tell me what they are going to charge and the service they provide,'" according to one marketing manager.

"Then," she continues, "another salesperson might call and ask about a competitor's standard terms and conditions, or what their marketing effort looks like, or how they sell a product in a particular region."

A strategist for a large electronics company confirmed the hot line's value: "The hot line," he stated, "enabled our sales force to make many sales they might otherwise have lost."

Making the Hot Line Work

To work effectively, the hot line must invite questions as much as it solicits information. Your contacts in the field need information to do their job better. The most successful hot lines work well because they not only receive timely information, but dispense it as well.

Speed and accuracy are also hot-line requirements. "If you can provide your field force with solid information, quickly and efficiently," the Digital manager said, emphatically, "then people will flock to use it. We aimed for a fast response to hot-line questions. As a result, there were times when we received more information and requests then we could handle."

"After our initial success, the news about this hot line spread mostly by word of mouth."

How can you publicize your hot line and get it off to a running start? Try the following methods that other managers have found successful:

• *Training programs.* "We introduced the hot line and our group's overall intelligence-gathering efforts through our regional training programs," recalls one manager. "Each of our employee-training programs contained a section on the competition. The hot line was mentioned here.

"Our sales force received word of our services through an audiotape training program. Since they were already being trained via tape, we just piggybacked our message about the hot line onto their standard training curriculum."

• *Internal publications.* Another manager publishes a quarterly analysis that describes the competition and any new entrants. The hot line was advertised in that report. "Our companywide magazine also mentioned this special service," the manager said.

• *Networking.* "There were other hot lines scattered around Digital," said the Digital marketing manager. "We started informing them of our existence. They quickly spread the word."

Developing and Maintaining the Hot Line

To insure that you provide your callers with the best possible information, you need to know why they are calling, the type of information they need, and the depth of information you can supply.

These are the steps you should follow to make sure your hot line succeeds:

1. Log all calls received either in a book or onto a data base.
2. Track the specific requests and incoming information by type.
3. Locate the hot line near the competitor files or information base.
4. Have the hot line staffed by professionals, at least part-time.
5. Those manning the hot line should, from time to time, meet with its prime users to refine, or redefine, its usefulness.
6. Follow up all hot-line inquiries to see if a particular caller's needs were met. Record all successes for use in promoting the hot line.

By logging all calls, you will be able to see just how effective the hot line is. In addition, you will be able to spot trends in the types of questions asked or the information supplied. Finally, by tracking numbers of requests and their responses, you will be better able to justify any additional staffing needs, should the demand call for it.

Electronic Mail

Electronic or voice mail can quickly unite the intelligence seeker and supplier. At many of the high-tech companies I have visited, employees use their electronic mail systems almost as much as they do their telephones.

A manager of market intelligence at Hewlett-Packard has reaped tremendous benefits from his electronic mail system. "By broadcasting my information need on the mail system, I have picked up information on how many disk drives a vendor may be manufacturing for a competitor or how many power supplies he is producing and who the OEM is."

To make his electronic mail system work for him, he has established

MONITORING SNAPSHOT 8

A Hot Line Form

You should record any calls taken on the hot line. A form similar to the one below can be used to record the reason for the call, as well as the information sources used to answer the caller's questions.

Date:_____   Time:_____

Caller Name:_____   Department:_____

Telephone:_____   Staff Initials:_____

****

Question Posed:_____

_____

_____

_____

_____

_____

_____

///

To be filled out following the request:

   Which sources proved best for answering the above question:

    ___Central Files   ___In-house Expert_____

    ___Data Base   ___Library

    ___Other_____

Notes: _____
             _____
             _____
             _____

(©1985, Information Data Search)

a broad network of contacts throughout Hewlett-Packard. For each contact, he has a mailbox number. "I probably have 600 or 700 people on my network. Figure each of them, in turn, may pass my message along to 15 or so other people. I have a lot of visibility as a result."

"I have achieved some minor intelligence-gathering miracles through the electronic mail service. For instance, I once needed information on a certain competitor's overseas suppliers. Only days after I broadcast my request over the mail system, someone sent back information on how many disk drives a vendor is building for a competitor. This information, in turn, gave us a lead on the number of computers the competitor is truly building."

Competitor-Reporting Forms

A competitor-reporting form is an effective intelligence-gathering tool that can be distributed beyond the confines of the sales force.

Competitor-reporting forms serve to identify specific competitor information that might otherwise become lost in standard sales call reports or other standard corporate reports.

According to Christopher Ritz, the distribution consultant mentioned earlier, Anheuser-Busch requires its sales force to fill out a competitor-activity report at the end of each week. The reports may contain information on competitors' pricing or reports of under-the-table deals. Anheuser-Busch maintains a library of these files for future reference.

A general rule of thumb for the design of such forms: Keep them simple, and list only one or two questions. Don't clutter up the form with a myriad of questions. Instead, select the one or two key questions to which you really need answers. In addition, spice the form with a special logo or color scheme that will appear both professional and eye-catching.

On the following page, you will see a sample reporting form produced by Abbott Laboratories that follows these basic guidelines.

The Intelligence Rep

A powerful way to increase the flow of intelligence is to establish intelligence representatives in different departments. The reps are volunteers

MONITORING SNAPSHOT 9

Spotlighting Intelligence

A marketing manager at Abbott Labs distributes his competitor-reporting forms to many sales and other executives at his company. To avoid having these executives lose their forms, he decided to add a little graphic punch to the page. In addition, he changed the form's original corporate blue color to a jazzy, dazzling hot red. Would you find this form hard to lose in your in box?

FOCUS
on
Competitive and Industry Intelligence

I have learned the following: Please add this to your files.
My source is:_____ (optional)
(Either attach information to this form or indicate below.)

From:_____ Date:_____
☐ Please send me more forms
Abbott Laboratories Diagnostics Division

who agree to devote a small portion of their time to gathering information and attending intelligence meetings.

Managers at one health-products company have appointed intelligence-gathering reps throughout their various product lines. These reps meet once each quarter to exchange information on the competition. Each rep has usually gathered certain pieces of information not known by the rest of the group. When the reps meet to exchange information, the result is that each rep then goes back to his respective group with far more information that he started out with.

A rep can be almost anyone—a salesperson, buyer, actuary, or research scientist. He or she should have been with the company or in the industry for a while, and should be a good "people" person. Those qualities aside, the most important trait to look for in a rep is eagerness to help. Other important traits a rep should have include

- Good listening ability
- Persistence
- Attentiveness to detail
- Insatiable curiosity
- Congeniality
- Ability to think clearly

The rep system is a way to formalize intelligence gathering without much cost. It does require a lot of "care and feeding" from the intelligence coordinator, however. You must be sure to give the reps regular rewards for information—anything from a "thank you," to letters to their bosses, to giving them information they can use in their jobs.

As well, you need to let reps know how the information they provide is helping the company. If the rep feels his information just vanishes into the black hole of the strategic planning process, he will not feel motivated to collect more data.

It is also important to use your reps sparingly. The reps have other jobs and could easily find intelligence demands too great.

Once you have developed a network of reps, you should publish a directory and give it to all the reps. This gives each of them a network of contacts and can be a valuable tool for them.

In addition, plan periodic, but brief, meetings among reps so they can meet each other and share ideas and information. You can also schedule "emergency" brainstorming sessions with selected reps if you need to gather information on a particular competitor or a particular market.

One food company successfully expedited the rep-recruiting process by having their champion send a note to department heads, requesting that they appoint reps.

The Intelligence Audit

Hot lines, electronic mail, and reporting forms will not uncover all the competitor information housed within your company. You may discover that soon after you begin to tap your organization's more obvious intelligence assets—the R&D or sales departments, for example—you will have to actively dig out other valuable, yet hidden, information resources. The best way to uncover these resources is by conducting an intelligence audit.

An intelligence audit is an inventory of your company's intelligence assets. These assets include private competitor files, individually constructed data bases, scattered market studies purchased outside the library, as well as names of industry and competitor experts within your company.

Once you have decided to begin an audit, you will want to move slowly. You have a better chance of succeeding with a small audit and a far greater chance of failing if you immediately take the audit company-wide. Start by testing the audit on one department or one small division.

Starting Out

Your first task is to understand the information you need to collect. One way is to conduct an imaginary intelligence audit of each department's intelligence resources.

Do what I did for the fictitious purchasing department on the following page (Monitoring Snapshot 10). I let my mind's eye wander through the department. I then jotted down all the printed resources I saw on their shelves. These resources included competitor product catalogs, credit reports, and so on. I also postulated what competitor information each of these resources contained. This activity helped me better understand the questions I wanted to ask both of purchasing and of other departments as I proceeded through the audit.

MONITORING SNAPSHOT 10

Conducting an Imaginary Audit

Pick a department you know well in your organization. Then let your mind's eye wander through it, picking out information sources located inside it. On a scrap of paper, list all the sources you come across. You may be surprised at how intelligence-rich many organizations are. Take a look at the sample below. See how this purchasing department contained all sorts of competitor information, including competitor product catalogs, credit reports, and private files.

Department Selected For An Audit: *PURCHASING*

SOURCE:	INTELLIGENCE CONTAINED:
COMPETITOR'S CATALOGS	— *PRODUCT LINE*
	— *PRICING*
	— *DISTRIBUTION CENTERS*
CREDIT REPORTS	— *COMPETITOR'S SALES*
	— *COMPETITOR'S LIQUIDITY/ OUTSTANDING DEBT*
	— *COMPETITOR'S OFFICERS*
MR. SMITH'S FILES	— *INDUSTRY ARTICLES*
	— *ASSOCIATION STATISTICS*
	— *MARKETING STANDINGS*
	— *COMPANY POLICY STATEMENTS*
	— *LATEST PATENTS*

Designing an Audit Questionnaire

You may have to design a different audit questionnaire for each department you speak to. Because the information you need may vary for each department, your questions may change as well.

Your audit should have two major objectives:

• **Objective 1:** *Locating physical resources.* You should be looking for miscellaneous file cabinets, market studies, internal memos, and so forth. You need to hunt down where the intelligence itself physically lies.

• **Objective 2:** *Locating intellectual resources.* Your company is very likely full of experts who have particular areas of knowledge that can be useful in competitor monitoring. Besides taking inventory of these experts, you should try to find out more about their areas of expertise. For example, you need to ask questions about the trade shows they attend and which competitors they know best.

There are several steps involved in taking an audit. These steps include:

• **Step 1:** *Champion's support.* While not absolutely necessary, it will make your job a lot easier if your champion can help you gain the support of other key executives, or if he can mandate participation in an audit. One food-manufacturing company I have worked with is having the company president write a letter to all those participating in the audit. That single letter, sent under his signature, has opened up a lot of doors and made the audit's successful outcome all the more likely.

• **Step 2:** *Create a list.* Make a list of all departments you feel would be prime candidates for an audit.

• **Step 3:** *Schedule appointments.* Arrange appointments to meet individually or collectively with representatives from each department to discuss your overall intelligence goals for the audit. This group can help you iron out or anticipate problems that you might encounter when conducting the audit.

In just such a meeting I participated in recently, all the potential interviewers for the audit, representing groups from throughout the client's company, critiqued a sample questionnaire. The result: At the end of the meeting, we had a much better, more workable questionnaire.

• **Step 4:** *Design the test questionnaire.* Design the test questionnaire with the format and ranking of questions that you feel will work.

Below are potential topics for the questionnaire:

• experts and their expertise
• private files and contents
• private library collections
• magazine and newsletter subscriptions
• schedule of regular meetings and topics discussed
• trade shows regularly attended
• type of intelligence needed by the department
• format in which information should be communicated
• how information supplied will be used

• **Step 5:** *Execute questionnaire:* Do not expect to hand respondents a copy of the blank questionnaire to fill out. It is up to you or those interviewers you appoint to ask the questions and fill out the forms.

Beware of Audit Failure!

Use an intelligence audit only if you have developed a means of storing the information you collect (see the next chapter for details on organizing intelligence). If you simply collect the information but lack adequate means to process it once it arrives, you may be the victim of "audit failure."

A marketing executive with one of the major television broadcasting networks told me this story of audit failure:

One day, a group of the company's top marketing executives decided they wanted some comprehensive files of all company activities . . . information on sales prospects, all forms of company activities.

We spread the word throughout the company and provided a secretary and a means of storing the information in a combination manual file and data base.

Before long, we were inundated—swamped with responses. The office that had taken on the job of coordinating and collecting all the data simply could not keep up with the influx of information.

Requests could not be responded to quickly enough. We were getting caught in a vicious cycle: receiving too much information too quickly and then not being able to pump out the answers. There was always a problem of quality control, as well. No one could say how accurate or true a piece of information was.

CHAPTER 5

STORING INTELLIGENCE:
Is the Computer the Answer?

If you have followed the steps described in previous chapters, you have collected a great deal of competitor information. You might have to act on some of this information immediately, in which case you will store it in a readily accessible desk file drawer. But if you are monitoring more than two or three companies and if you want to provide information to a range of users, you will need much more than one file drawer. You will need a system to store the information so that you can easily access it later on, and so that others in the company can use it.

You have many options when it comes to storing competitor information. Depending on your monitoring program's scope, breadth, and funding, you can choose a simple manual file system, a combination of manual and computerized storage, or a totally computerized system.

Several large companies, such as Motorola and Kodak, have built large textual data bases to store intelligence for their companywide monitoring programs. These data bases have at best a spotty track record, and because they require enormous cash outlays, are an option only for a Fortune-500 company. Smaller companies or divisions of larger corporations must use hardcopy files, but they can effectively supplement those files with computerized spreadsheets or indexes. Becton-Dickinson and the MAC Group are examples of companies that have harnessed the best of manual files and computers to organize their competitor information.

This chapter will help you decide which is the best information-storage system for your competitor-monitoring program. It includes examples of both successful and unsuccessful data-storage programs, and analyzes why they succeeded or failed.

MANUAL FILES

Most companies with sophisticated computer software to store competitor information also maintain manual competitor files. Even so, certain companies use their files more effectively than others. The most effective manual file systems have these two characteristics:

• *A mix of internal and external sources.*   Each competitor file contains both internal documents, including memos, strategic reports, and market assessments, and external documents, such as annual reports, SEC reports, newspaper articles, and published market studies.

• *An effective index.*   The files are not only indexed alphabetically by company, but are also cross-indexed by subject area. For example, instead of just listing *Bank of America,* an effective index would also list *Bank of America* under *Cash Management Systems, Retail Banking Products,* and so on. This allows the researcher to locate all the important information that might otherwise be lost.

Bill Sammon, author of *Business Competitor Intelligence* (Wiley, 1984) and a strategic planner for Pfizer, has used an index to his department's competitor files both to organize and to communicate intelligence. The index, which organizes competitor files by company name and by area of business, is distributed to a host of managers at Pfizer. "I found that the index is a communications tool for our managers," commented Sammon. "Because of the index, people come to the files and use the materials, which did not happen as much as before the index.

Often, once managers start reviewing a particular file's contents, they find the file lacking certain information and let us know what exactly we needed to add to it for the future. This has helped build our files into an extremely useful resource."

In sharp contrast to Sammon's experience, I witnessed a file disaster at a large telecommunications company. A strategic planner, given the task of organizing his company's monitoring program, assembled a set of competitor files. The files contained only the most basic public information about the competition, such as annual reports and investment reports. His files lacked internal documents and even major news articles that had appeared on the competition.

The outcome: His files were rarely used and rarely updated. Senior management bypassed his files entirely, relying instead on the files found in the legal department.

What Your Competitor Files Should Contain

Too many people pack their files with useless documents, papers that serve no one's needs and just take up valuable space. Useless information can hamper a search for valuable information. Competitor files should provide insights on competitors rather than covering old ground. Your competitor files should be designed to meet your constituency's specific information needs.

The listing below presents a fairly complete selection of sources (although you may not find listed here those that are unique to your industry). You must decide what kinds of intelligence you need most and select your sources accordingly.

External Sources

Public Sources (exclusively for publicly traded companies):

1.   Annual reports
2.   Securities and Exchange Commission (SEC) reports

Public Sources (for both privately held and publicly traded companies)

1.   News articles
2.   Product literature and catalogs

3. Price lists
4. Market studies
5. Business school case studies
6. General public filings

A fairly complete list of these filings is presented in Chapter 2.

Internal Sources

The following is a list of internal documents that you may want to keep in your competitor files:

1. Memos
2. Strategic plans
3. Sales-call reports
4. Hot-line inquiries
5. Competitor reports
6. Product evaluations (R&D reports)

An intelligence audit can help you locate additional internal documents, as well as important external information that others have collected.

The Care and Feeding of Your Files

If you maintain files for many users, you must monitor these files carefully. Otherwise, you will lose control of your collection.

Maintaining your competitor files is not much different from maintaining your family tax records. Let it go a little, and you will be in trouble (just remember those nightmarish days before April 15, when you couldn't find the receipts you knew you had somewhere). Keep up with your competitor files on a regular basis and they will be relatively easy to manage.

Here are some tips on maintaining and developing your maturing files:

• *Identify your files' major users.* Are they marketing managers, sales reps, scientists, or top executives? Match the information you collect to the file users' needs before you spend countless hours clipping and filing useless documents.

For example, if you were to design a competitor file to serve your company's R&D executives, you should collect and file a great deal of technical literature. You would not necessarily need to clip and file *Business Week* articles. The general business press is probably of less interest to your company scientists than are articles on recent patent filings.

• *Learn which competitor files are called for most often.*   For instance, are your file's customers calling only for the same six files all the time? Are the remaining 30 files left virtually untouched? At this point, you should seriously consider eliminating the remaining 30 files.

• *Learn which portions of each competitor file are reviewed most frequently.*   Are users just taking annual reports? Or do they only want to examine news articles and special market reports? Examination of file usage may indicate the need to educate others about the additional material in the file, or to seek out new sources.

To track how your competitor files are being used and who is using them, and to find out whether they are meeting your monitoring program's needs, take the following steps:

First, have the file's users sign a log sheet for everything they remove from the files.

Second, after the first few months of operation, check to see which departments are using the files most frequently. A quick check of the log book will tell you this.

Third, survey a sample of users, and ask them two basic questions: Which file materials did you find most useful? What sources were the files lacking?

DATA BASES

When should you go electronic? That is the big question for many managers who track the competition. This section will help you decide when to start a competitor data base and what kind of data base to build in the first place. It will also show you how to design a data base that complements your manual files.

Those executives who have built successful competitor data bases use the computer to:

1.   Provide easy access to data for many users.

2.   Locate competitor information that can easily get lost in corporate archives. (See the Kraft example described in Chapter 7.)

3.   Locate and cross-index their company's experts. (See the Kodak example below.)

4.   Add more value to the information they collect by having the data base extrapolate trends from raw data. (See the MAC Group's data base below.)

Varieties of Competitor Data Bases

I have seen three basic types of competitor-intelligence data bases: spreadsheets, directories, and those that provide text and analysis. Each is useful in different situations, and some intelligence departments use all three.

In this section, I will examine each of the three major formats and present examples of how certain companies have succeeded or failed in applying them to their monitoring programs.

Format 1: Spreadsheets

Microcomputer-based spreadsheets are by far the most prevalent type of competitor data base. Spreadsheets are simple to format and flexible enough to meet many needs. And, since most spreadsheets can be stored in a microcomputer, a manager can design a data base of his own choosing—without having to go through cumbersome corporate committees for approval. As a result, the spreadsheet data bases are among the most creative, up-to-date, and productive of the lot.

THE SIMPLE MAC GROUP APPROACH TO DATA BASES

The following two spreadsheets produced at the MAC Group, a Cambridge, Massachusetts-based consulting firm, demonstrate how much value can be packed into a small data base.

Each MAC data base works because it has a clear goal and a simple concept. And because each is so simple, it takes little time to maintain. Charles Green, a MAC vice-president and the data-base designer, estimates he spends no more than $1,000 worth of his time during the year gathering and entering the data.

Data Base 1: Marketshare

In the management-consulting world, the number of professional employees is an indication of a firm's revenues. This relationship inspired Green to construct a marketshare data base by estimating the number of employees at rival consulting firms.

As you can see from the sample he submitted, he estimates a major competitor's (MAR) compounded growth rate of its employee base from 1982 through 1986 as 37.5 percent. During that same period, a second major competitor's (LA) growth rate was only 6.1 percent. (Please note: All names and numbers have been disguised to maintain confidentiality.)

The information used to compile this data base comes from over 75 different sources, including recruiting literature, magazine articles, MAC's alumni network, and plain industry gossip.

Data Base 2: Management Structure

Green's second data base lists management consultants recently hired from the nation's leading business schools. By listing which schools MAC's competing firms are hiring from, this data base gives the MAC Group a number of important bits of strategic information about its competition. The data base reveals which schools are a particular competitor's current favorites, which in turn can reveal the firm's management philosophy (Harvard and MIT, for example, have different approaches to business management). The data base can also provide a simple tally of new hiring, which indicates growth rates at the respective firms.

The information for this data base is drawn from alumni listings published by the business schools themselves. Green collects each year's alumni listing and enters it onto the spreadsheet.

BECTON-DICKINSON CHARTS TECHNOLOGY

A market analyst with a subsidiary of Becton-Dickinson, a health products company, has built a small spreadsheet data base that gives her a quick review of competitors' latest diagnostic tests. The data base contains information on approximately 60 companies. It is simple, takes only one hour each week to update, and is easily accessible.

This analyst draws on an eclectic group of sources to update and maintain the data base. These sources include information gleaned from professional and scientific meetings, patent searches, and various

MONITORING SNAPSHOT 11

A Marketshare Spreadsheet

A senior manager at the MAC Group, a management-consulting firm, has compiled competitors' marketshares from employment estimates received from his company's recruiters, alumni information, and even industry gossip. (Note: Actual firm names are disguised.)

WORLDWIDE GENERAL MANAGEMENT CONSULTING INDUSTRY NUMBER OF PROFESSIONALS

YEAR	IND. TOTAL	CARNA-TION	HLD	SEER	SMITH	LA	EXT	MAC GRP	MAR	XYZ
86	6185	1850	1000	55	225	155	1400	380	1000	120
85	5666	1800	993	50	200	153	1250	360	750	110
84	5075	1680	950	40	185	148	1080	350	550	92
83	4559	1530	980	35	150	124	930	335	400	75
82	4203	1450	930	30	120	123	890	320	280	60
81	3884	1365	900	28	97	109	840	300	190	55
80	3627	1300	830	20	75	94	800	260	200	48
79	3282	1244	750	16	60	82	760	230	105	35
78	3015	1145	700	15	50	70	700	240	70	25
77	2707	1064	650	10	35	56	650	180	42	20

COMPOUND ANNUAL GROWTH RATES:

FR. '78	9.4%	6.2%	4.6%	17.6%	20.7%	10.5%	9.1%	5.9%	39.4%	21.7%
FR. '80	9.3%	6.1%	3.2%	18.4%	20.1%	8.6%	9.8%	6.5%	30.8%	16.5%
FR. '82	10.1%	6.3%	1.8%	16.4%	17.0%	6.1%	12.0%	4.4%	37.5%	18.9%

MARKET SHARES

YEAR	IND. TOTAL	CAR-NATION	HLD	SECR	SMITH	LA	EXT	MAC GRP	MAR	XYZ
86	100.0%	29.9%	16.2%	0.9%	3.6%	2.5%	22.6%	6.1%	16.2%	1.9%
85	100.0%	31.8%	17.5%	0.9%	3.5%	2.7%	22.1%	6.4%	13.2%	1.9%
84	100.0%	33.1%	18.7%	0.8%	3.6%	2.9%	21.3%	6.9%	10.8%	1.8%
83	100.0%	33.6%	21.5%	0.8%	3.3%	2.7%	20.4%	7.3%	8.8%	1.6%
82	100.0%	34.5%	22.1%	0.7%	2.9%	2.9%	21.2%	7.6%	6.7%	1.4%
81	100.0%	35.1%	23.2%	0.7%	2.5%	2.8%	21.6%	7.7%	4.9%	1.4%
80	100.0%	35.8%	22.9%	0.6%	2.1%	2.6%	22.1%	7.2%	5.5%	1.3%
79	100.0%	37.9%	22.9%	0.5%	1.8%	2.5%	23.2%	7.0%	3.2%	1.1%
78	100.0%	38.0%	23.2%	0.5%	1.7%	2.3%	23.2%	8.0%	2.3%	0.8%
77	100.0%	39.3%	24.0%	0.4%	1.3%	2.1%	24.0%	6.6%	1.6%	0.7%

Notes:
  Company data are disguised.
  Sources—approx. 75, ranging from recruiting literature to magazine articles to alumni to gossip.
  Methodology—subjective interpolation aimed at reducing aggregate level of contradictions in source data.

MONITORING SNAPSHOT 12

Watching How Your Competitor Grows

The information displayed here shows how one manager at the MAC Group has successfully built a data base to track a competitors' hiring trends and organization shifts. The source used here is the Harvard Business School alumni directory.

HBS Alumni at Competitors

Source—HBS 85–86 Directory; Sorted by Year, Employer, City

City	Employer	Class of	Last Name	First Name
London	Bain	85	C.	Ian
Boston	Bain	85	D.	Margaret
Boston	Bain	85	Q.	Adalene
Boston	Bain	85	L.	Lynn
S.F.	Bain	85	B.	David
Boston	Bain	85	J.	David
Boston	Bain	85	B.	Theodore
Boston	Bain	85	A.	Anthony Simon
Boston	Bain	85	S.	Paul
Boston	Bain	85	S.	Judith
Boston	Bain	85	L.	Aaron
Boston	Bain	85	C.	Levon
Boston	Bain	85	B.	Gail
Boston	Bain	85	C.	Ramos
Boston	Bain	85	H.	Randall
Boston	Bain	85	F.	Susan
Boston	Bain	85	B.	Daniel
NYC	BCG	85	B.	Thomas
London	BCG	85	A.	Christopher
NYC	BCG	85	D.	Ashley
Boston	BCG	85	L.	Alexander
London	BCG	85	A.	S.Marcus
London	BCG	85	W.	M.Jonathan
London	BCG	85	R.	David
Boston	BCG	85	L.	Carl
Chicago	Booz	85	G.	Jonathan
NYC	Booz	85	G.	Gretchen
NYC	Booz	85	D.	Janice
Chicago	Booz	85	G.	Stephen
Chicago	Booz	85	M.	Margaret
Chicago	Booz	85	B.	Peter
Chicago	Booz	85	G.	Scott
NYC	Booz	85	C.	Charles
Boston	MAC	85	T.	Kee Hian
Chicago	MAC	85	W.	Richard
London	McKinsey	85	W.	Johanna
NYC	McKinsey	85	B.	Varun
NYC	McKinsey	85	P.	David
NYC	McKinsey	85	C.	D.Gordon
NYC	McKinsey	85	B.	Mary
NYC	McKinsey	85	M.	Guy
NYC	McKinsey	85	K.	Cynthia
NYC	McKinsey	85	E.	Petter
NYC	McKinsey	85	C.	J.Michael
D.C.	McKinsey	85	K.	Patrick
London	McKinsey	85	G.	Colin
NYC	McKinsey	85	P.	Chris
D.C.	SPA	85	W.	Adrian
D.C.	SPA	85	S.	Wylie

government-required corporate compliance reports, such as the FDA's 510K filing. She also maintains manual files containing this information.

A printout of her data base is distributed quarterly. According to the analyst, her data base has become so widely used that almost no one uses the manual files anymore.

"I use it constantly to help R&D," the analyst reports. "For example, I use the data base to report Cetus Corporation's new publications, new patents, or new products. This kind of information keeps our R&D department tuned to the marketplace and one jump ahead of the competitors."

OTHER SPREADSHEETS YOU CAN BUILD

Here are ideas for other competitor-monitoring spreadsheets that you can construct:

1. *Price-comparison data base.* A spreadsheet is an excellent way to compare competitors' products and prices. By placing competitors'

MONITORING SNAPSHOT 13

Tracking Technology by Spreadsheet

An analyst at Becton-Dickinson has assembled the latest product-development information on 60 of Becton-Dickinson's competitors. This compact spreadsheet is used regularly by the R&D staff to keep on top of trends and competitor activity. The information for this data base comes from professional meetings as well as from official government filings.

```
Filename: COMPETIT
Diskette: Lotus Files Vol 2

                         COMPETITOR INFORMATION - CHLAMYDIA
-------------------------------------------------------------------------------
COMPANY                  TEST                          COMMENTS/ SOURCE(S)
-------------------------------------------------------------------------------
EXAMPLES (ficticious info):

Time Diagnostics         DFA - Antigen detection       Kit at Research Center; 510 (k) at Research Center;
                                                         Research done by Diagnostics Rouge of France

Sclavic Diagnostici      EIA - Not known whether antigen or antibody  Available in Europe only; patent at Research
                            detection                    Center; looking for marketer in U.S
                                                       Source:  Biotechnology News 5/9/86

Scottish Laboratories    Scotticult - Culture & ID Kit  Presented poster at '86 Am. Microbiology Meeting
                                                         on purification of 60K membrane protein
```

©1986 Becton-Dickinson Company. Reprinted with permission.

prices next to yours, you can uncover revealing trends in competitors' pricing strategies. For example, you may discover that your competitors are dropping prices on a seasonal basis, or changing prices in reaction to your market moves.

2. *Product or service comparisons.* A spreadsheet allows detailed comparisons of product features, and thus highlights the features of your competitors' products that differ from your company's product. The spreadsheet permits easier side-by-side comparison of features than would separate reports on each product.

3. *Other trends.* Spreadsheets can help you identify trends in almost any measurable variable, including sales, production, number of employees (as you saw in the MAC data base), square footage of plants, or number of locations.

Format 2: Directory/Index

A good computerized index or directory can speed access to information by instantly telling users which file to consult or which expert to call. Microcomputer data-base management software, such as DBase III[tm] or RBase[tm], are widely used for this application and can produce powerful indexes.

As Monitoring Snapshot 14 shows, a product researcher at an electronic-parts manufacturer created an index to help match hundreds of competitors' parts with those of her own company. This index allowed for the first time a clear comparison of competitors' product lines. It also steered users to the file containing the hardcopy of each competitor's product sheet.

A Directory of New Hires

At the request of a marketing manager, the human resources department at a large industrial service company maintains a data base of new hires who also used to work for the competition.

Each month the department prints a list of the latest new hires, usually truck drivers or salespeople. The marketing manager then telephones the new company employees to debrief them.

"The information given is not confidential or proprietary in any way," states the manager, "but it does help me confirm suspicions about the

MONITORING SNAPSHOT 14

Competitor Index Power

In this brief description, a market analyst for an electronic parts firm describes how her index is used to pull together product information from hundreds of pieces of product literature on file. For the first time this index allowed a product managers to make a comprehensive comparison of competitors' products with their firm's own.

MULTI-NATIONAL ACCOUNTS GROUP

COMPETITION FILE CROSS-REFERENCE

This cross-reference has been handled in the following manner:

I have gone through every company we have information on from the competition file and noted what kind of products they manufacture. These companies are listed by product lines according to the content page of the ***** Full-Line Catalog. Therefore, if you are looking for a list of potential competitors for our Pin and Socket line, this cross-reference outlines the companies you should look for.

Files with a pink label contain corporate information, annual reports, correspondence between ***** employees dealing with the company, advertising. Yellow labeled files contain any cross reference information we may have between that company's products and our products. All files with green labels contain competitive catalog information.

You are welcome to help yourself to any information you need; we only ask that you return it when you are through.

TABLE OF CONTENTS

CONNECTOR TYPE	PAGE
PIN AND SOCKET CONNECTORS	
& HIGH CURRENT COMPONENTS	2
D-SUBMINIATURE CONNECTORS	3
TERMINALS	5
PRINTED CIRCUIT BOARD	
INTERCONNECTION SYSTEMS	6
.100" x .100" CONNECTORS	7
SHUNTS	8
RIBBON CABLE CONNECTORS	9
INSULATION DISPLACEMENT PRODUCTS	10
CABLE PRODUCTS	11
TOOLING (APPLICATION & MACHINES)	12
FLAT FLEXIBLE CIRCUITRY CONNECTORS	13
EDGE CONNECTORS	14
SWITCHES (* = MEMBRANE)	16
SOCKETS	17
TELECOMMUNICATION PRODUCTS	19
DIN 41612 COMPATIBLE CONNECTORS	20
FIBER OPTIC CONNECTORS	21
COMPLIANT PIN/HDI TECHNOLOGY	22
CIRCULAR CONNECTORS (* = CIRCULAR DINS)	23
SURFACE MOUNT TECHNOLOGY	24
COAXIAL AND/OR FILTERED CONNECTORS	25
INTERFACE CABLE AND/OR IEEE 488 CONNECTORS	26

competition or inform me of impending changes at a particular competitor."

The data base, in operation for less than one year, has already given this manager a great deal of information that he and his management can act on. In addition, it has allowed him to build a network of contacts throughout the company fairly rapidly.

"Why build a data base for this purpose," you are probably asking, "when all human resources has to do each month is type a list of these names on a piece of paper? Why computerize?"

At this juncture, I would say your point is well taken. But what will happen in one or two years, when the list may grow into the hundreds or the thousands? This company could benefit greatly by creating an electronic data base that will cross-index these new hires by their previous employers, as well as by their areas of expertise.

MONITORING SNAPSHOT 15

New Hires Data Base

One inventive product manager arranged to have his company's personnel department generate monthly reports on his firm's new hires from information already in its personnel data base. This printout gives the manager a full list of all new hires and the competitors they used to work for. The manager then speaks to many of these employees about the competition.

New Hires Data Base

LAST NAME	FIRST	MIDDLE	COMPANY BRANCH	CURRENT JOB TITLE	DATE HIRED	PREVIOUS EMPLOYER	DATE OF EMPLOYMENT	PAST POSITION
Abrams	John	M	NE	Driver	1/05/87	CMS	9/79-12/86	Driver
Charles	Mark	D	SW	Marketing	1/05/87	DRI	10/84-1/87	Sales
Dross	Daniel	G	SW	Planning	1/05/87	HHT	7/81-12/86	Planning
Englehard	David	B	SW	Sales	1/05/87	DRI	6/81-12/86	Sales
Fox	Mark	B	SW	Engineering	1/02/87	CMS	6/81-12/86	Engineering
Gruber	Jane	S	E	Production	1/09/87	CMS	6/83-11/86	Manufacturing
Grupp	Michael	X	W	Driver	1/12/87	CMS	8/84-1/87	Driver
Hill	Barry	L	NW	Service	1/05/87	HHT	6/77-11/86	Service
Menges	ClarenceA		SW	Service	1/26/87	HHT	5/83-1/87	Sales
Pollak	LawrenceT		NE	Service	1/15/87	SSR	7/84-10/86	Service
Stein	Hillary	N	NE	Sales	1/15/87	SCM	9/85-7/86	Sales
Trump	Stanley	D	E	Sales	1/15/87	CMS	10/83-1/87	Sales

Other Directories You Can Build

There are dozens of other potential uses for an index or a directory in organizing competitor information. Consider these other possibilities:

1. *Directory of internal and external experts.* One large midwestern company is in the process of polling over 350 employees to develop a list of internal "experts" indexed by area of expertise. The experts are selected for their knowledge of specific companies, technologies, or markets. Ultimately, the organizers hope to track the trade shows the experts attend, the companies they are most knowledgeable about, the private files they maintain, and their areas of technical expertise.

Just as the above company has created a list of internal experts, you could create a listing of external contacts your executives have in the marketplace.

2. *Directory of internal data bases and private libraries.* You could create a directory of reports, market studies, and special competitor files owned by various executives around the company. In addition, you could catalog any private data bases the executives maintain on their personal floppy disks. The proliferation of microcomputers in the workplace has allowed executives to create their own miniature data bases. Of the thousands of floppy disks floating around major corporations, a significant proportion probably contain competitor data.

You may find that such a directory can identify unique intelligence sources, as well as help eliminate duplication of resources.

3. *Listing of subscription holders.* Compile a master listing of all trade and industry magazine- and newsletter-subscribers within your organization. The list can save your department or company money by allowing you to locate information quickly and avoid duplicate subscriptions. This is a perfect list for the corporate library to maintain.

4. *Sales force directory.* Create a cross-index of the sales force. The index could identify each individual by area of expertise, territory covered, type of customer contact, or industry expertise. By the same token, you may also want to index customer support engineers, service personnel, and any other groups which regularly deal with customers.

Format 3: Textual

A number of Fortune-500 companies—Motorola and Kodak among them—have begun to build large data bases containing huge volumes of text on competitors, technology, markets, and the general business climate. The vision these companies share is that employees companywide will be able to access the same body of information quickly and easily.

Debate about the value of the these systems is fierce, especially in light of their often mammoth costs. In this section I will examine data bases built by Kodak, Motorola, and others, highlighting the lessons to be learned from each.

MISTAKES TO AVOID: WHAT WENT WRONG AT HI-TECH, INC?

(A note to the reader: Hi-Tech, Inc. is a fictitious name. The company, which is actually the subject of this story, has requested that its name be disguised. Otherwise, all the other events reported here are undisguised).

Approximately seven years ago, Hi-Tech decided it needed a centralized source of competitor information. Senior staff wanted that information available in a computerized data base. Hi-Tech already had all the software and hardware necessary to make the data base work. All it had to do was supply the personnel to gather and enter the data. All this was accomplished. Yet, within a few years the data base was shelved.

How did this happen?

As the story unfolds, I would like you to reflect on your company's own experiences with data bases. How many of the problems Hi-Tech ran into are similar to your own? Also, ask yourself if they could have managed their data in some other way, a way that may have yielded better decision-making information for Hi-Tech's senior management.

The Beginning . . .   The impetus for a competitor data base at Hi-Tech was a companywide push for more consistent and more complete competitor analysis.

Senior management felt that competitor analysis had been disorganized, with each division using different standards and objectives from the others. Executives also said they needed more analysis, period. They felt they were seeing too much raw data and not enough sifting of this data to meet the increasingly competitive environment.

Hi-Tech believed the analysis to be important because it saw the marketplace of the 1980s as a tougher place to sell than that of the 1970s. It saw slower corporate growth, maturing markets, falling discretionary income, and pressure from its OEM buyers for price cuts.

Hi-Tech established a Management Information and Competitor Base (MICB) in the third quarter of 1980. "MICB was built," said a planner with Hi-Tech at the time, "to establish a focal point for Hi-Tech to collect and analyze competitive information and strategies. Specifically, we needed a centralized competitor data base for a variety of very practical reasons: First, many of our SBUs have common competitors, which would, on the surface, make a common data base an efficient tool. Second, our field force was not equipped to develop, maintain, and analyze a competitor data base. We could, therefore, not leave its maintenance to the divisional field force. Third, we needed an analysis of our total competitors, not just on an SBU level. That's why we felt we needed to place it at corporate. Fourth, we envisioned the data base as a tool that would be able to provide management and planners throughout Hi-Tech with competitor information available online and in hardcopy."

The Start-up . . .   A committee of eight managers was appointed to oversee the construction and formulation of MICB. Hi-Tech's senior corporate staff was targeted as the data base's main user.

Hi-Tech's out-of-pocket costs for establishing this data base proved negligible. The company already had the necessary hardware and software and made these available to the planner's group. The group was charged less than $10,000 for computer time at the end of the first year. The necessary personnel proved somewhat more expensive, but not exorbitant. It took a total of approximately one-and-one-half man-years to build the data base and approximately the same time to maintain it each year.

Selecting the Data . . .   A group of analysts were assigned to abstract and analyze raw data. Most of the news articles and annual reports they used were not entered in their full-text versions.

The management committee chose information from the following sources for the data base:

- Annual reports
- Trade associations

- Business reference services
- Books
- Business journals
- Primary research
- Sales-force, purchasing, R&D reports
- Local press
- Trade press
- Lawsuit disclosures
- Consultant reports
- Prospectuses
- Business literature indexes
- Government filings
- Internal corporate and SBU reports
- Customer feedback reports
- Distributor feedback reports
- Chamber-of-commerce reports

The Testing Period . . .   Hi-Tech began MICB in the third quarter of 1980. A trial version of the data base was developed by the second quarter of 1981. By September 1981, management made the MICB system available to the corporation.

In spring 1982, Hi-Tech reviewed the system and made changes based on the results gathered during the trial period.

By spring 1983, approximately two-and-one-half years after its founding, MICB's builders scheduled an overall review, a report card on the data base. The report card cast doubt on MICB and its overall usefulness. Senior management then decided to split the MICB data base up and give the appropriate portions to each of Hi-Tech's SBU's to manage and use. At present, not much is being done with MICB at any of the operating units.

Why Did Hi-Tech Shelve MICB?   MICB failed because it never met the needs of its primary audience. It tried to satisfy both senior management and SBU level needs at the same time. The result: There was too much detail for senior management and not enough for SBU level management.

The Lessons Learned . . . According to the planner, his staff learned the following lessons about constructing a competitor data base of any sort:

• Before you charge ahead, make sure you have carefully targeted specific groups that will use the data. Identify who they are and what information they need.

• Draw up a detailed operating plan that defines the data base's major audience, the personnel needed to maintain the data base, and the costs involved.

• Build the data base slowly. Do not rush into it. Check your progress often.

• Competitor analysis is the goal, not the retrieval system. The only reason to computerize information is for added convenience.

KODAK'S HYBRID DATA BASE

Kodak's system, as of this writing, is approximately three years old and has helped the competitive assessment process in a modest way, according to a manager in Kodak's marketing group.

The Kodak data base contains abstracts of news articles, as well as summaries of internally written competitive studies. The news articles selected for the data base cover both the markets Kodak competes in and the competitors in those markets. Any internal study catalogued by the data base also has the name of the study's author tacked onto it. Approximately 90 percent of the data base contains abstracted articles, while the other 10 percent contains internal studies.

What makes this data base unique is its linking of competitive subjects to an internal expert. It is a hybrid data base that essentially combines text with names of Kodak's internal experts. Usually the person who authored the research report is also the person who knows a great deal about the competitor or the industry discussed in the abstracted report.

According to the marketing manager, the data base is extremely useful to his staff, but it remains underutilized by other groups within Kodak. "It is mostly used by the core group here in the marketing department," he stated, "and has not been used by others in the company, such as manufacturing or engineering." He feels that use of the data base could be increased by raising other departments' awareness of the data base and its contents.

Another problem that he is currently solving is the loss of the manual files from which the computerized information is taken. "Until recently, anyone who submitted an article to the system was designated as the author and held onto the article. Unfortunately, the owner of the article often lost his copy. That meant we no longer had an original hardcopy of the full article. We are now starting to make copies of any article abstracted for the data base and placing that duplicate in a central file."

Kodak farms out the data entry to a local vendor, who abstracts the articles, enters the abstracts, and then uploads the information onto Kodak's computer system. The data entry costs Kodak more than $60,000 per year for approximately 5,000 articles.

All in all, this data base is far too expensive a solution for a small company, and may not even be cost-effective for a large corporation.

THE HIGH-VOLUME DATA BASE

In sharp contrast to the Kodak system, another major consumer-products manufacturer has generated a lot of interest in its data base. With approximately 300 inquiries and an average of 20 unsolicited reports fed into it weekly, this company's strategic intelligence system is well used.

Like Kodak, this firm's senior management strongly supports its data base, called Strategic Intelligence Base (SIB), and has backed it with the necessary money.

SIB analysts regularly enter articles from key trade magazines, such as "Appliance" magazine, other major business journals, the Wall Street Journal, and even articles from competitors' home-town newspapers. In addition, the SIB staff solicits competitor information from all parts of the company.

This firm also has a unique method of encouraging contributions to its data base. According to a manager in the department that maintains SIB, "Once a week we pull off all unsolicited information that has come into the system from around the world, and this information is sent to the chairman and vice-chairman along with the name of the contributor. Because top management sees who is contributing to the program, people have more incentive to provide information.

The information fed into SIB from the field is what distinguishes this system from either Kodak's or "Hi-Tech's" system, where most of the competitor data comes almost exclusively from published sources.

Unlike "Hi-Tech's" and Kodak's data bases, the SIB data base is used extensively by this company's three major operating divisions, primarily by their sales forces.

The costs for the SIB are approximately the same as for Kodak's data base. It takes two SIB staffers to enter the information. The abstracts attempt to include all the meat in each article or memo abstracted. Similar to Kodak, the SIB staff maintains a manual file and/or microfiche copies of the original documents referred to on the data base.

Another unique feature of the SIB system is how its management validates the information entered into it. If unverified information comes from one source, SIB's analysts label the piece of news as a rumor. If it is verified by at least two sources, it is considered a fact, and identified as such. After a time, if a rumor is not verified or if it is found to be false, the attending staff removes it from the data base.

Still, a big question remains: Has SIB given the company a competitive advantage? In answer to this question, the SIB manager said that the system has given management one place where they can get an overview of the market and of the competition. He was hard-pressed, though, to say if the data base was responsible for any strategic or tactical victories.

MOTOROLA'S ELECTRONIC LIBRARY

Motorola has probably dedicated more dollars and more staff toward building its strategic intelligence system than any other company in America today. The annual budget for developing the intelligence system and supporting the personnel and equipment approaches one million dollars.

Motorola's data base, MIRIS (Motorola Intelligence Research Information System), attempts to monitor not just the competition, but also the entire business, political, and economic environment for the company's worldwide interests. This broad scope dictates that Motorola's data base must receive information from thousands of sources. Some of these sources are Motorola staff members; others come from outside the company. These outside sources include both articles and commercial data bases.

From the outset, Motorola decided to develop its information system in totally electronic form. This means that Motorola has no traditional corporate library, and virtually all the competitor information collected is entered into the MIRIS data base.

While Motorola claims some successes that are directly attributable to MIRIS, it also believes that the system has fallen short in delivering what was originally promised. In a series of discussions that I have had with Motorola's intelligence department over the years, the staff described the potential that MIRIS may someday fulfill; they also listed the pitfalls they fell into along the way.

The Inception . . .   In 1983, Motorola began assembling a team of intelligence analysts with diverse backgrounds. This analytical-research group is composed of people with specialities in political science, economics, technology, government, and business. They regularly review articles in both industry and general publications and conduct customized research for managers within Motorola. They are also MIRIS's major users.

In 1984, Motorola purchased a software package for approximately $100,000 to drive the MIRIS data base. The intelligence staff then began to develop agreements with a number of online commercial data-base vendors to download some of their data into MIRIS. Today MIRIS has approximately 55,000 records, with over 80 percent of the records coming directly from online data-base searches. The other 20 percent comes from in-house reports, newsletters, and market studies.

To insure that the printed reports and studies are entered onto MIRIS in a timely manner, the intelligence department has purchased a Kurzweil optical scanner that will read and electronically enter text directly into MIRIS.

What is the cost for all this technology? I estimate the MIRIS budget to be approximately $300,000 per year, including all hardware, software, information sources, and personnel. This is a large sum for any corporation to spend on a data base. What has MIRIS delivered to date?

On the Plus Side . . .   The MIRIS data has been used to analyze manufacturing-plant site selection options, and to analyze the risks of conducting business in various countries. MIRIS also has been used to analyze acquisition candidates, some of which have been purchased by Motorola, and to evaluate potential business partners. These evaluations have helped management decide whether Motorola should join forces with a prospective company on a joint venture.

Motorola also uses MIRIS to review regularly the latest data on certain countries and specific competitors. One case in point: Motorola's intelligence staff had been monitoring one of its competitors in Southeast Asia for almost a half a year. At that time, the information coming from MIRIS revealed to staff members that the competitor had executed a successful new market strategy in not one, but two, countries within the past six months. Until the MIRIS data base was used, Motorola was not even sure the competitor had a strategic initiative in Southeast Asia. As soon as MIRIS revealed the pattern, analysts informed management that they should develop counter-moves in that region.

But Problems Have Arisen . . .   There is a negative side, however, one that other companies should be made aware of. The data base, after three years of development, still is used by only a limited group outside the intelligence group.

Motorola's original goal was to make the data base available to anyone who needed information: planners, marketers, laboratory researchers, and others. Motorola has not yet been able to achieve that. The system has not come up as quickly as the company had hoped. The reasons for some of MIRIS' problems are two-fold: One, Motorola's efforts in building MIRIS is a pioneering one; two, Motorola's full-scale development of MIRIS has only recently been completed.

It is uncertain whether MIRIS will ever be able to reach the entire organization. Although there are 5,000 terminals worldwide in Motorola, the company is concerned that proprietary information may leak out of the system to foreign governments and competitors. Because of such security concerns, Motorola has had to build a security hierarchy and compartmentalization feature into MIRIS. This has also slowed down MIRIS's overall development, and limited access to a few users.

For now the Motorola MIRIS data base is a unique experiment. Because of its size and expense, it is likely to remain unique for many more years.

ADVANTAGES AND DISADVANTAGES OF TEXTUAL DATA BASES

Once a textual data base is up and running, it can provide its users with a great deal of information. Yet the road you must take to make a textual data base work is full of pitfalls. You must weigh all of these pitfalls against the potential benefits. You must ask yourself: In light of my company's available budget, staff and overall corporate objectives, does a textual data base make sense? Or, should I consider other data bases and manual file options?

The Advantages . . .

• *Companywide access.* A textual data base on a mainframe system can be distributed to the entire company via satellite terminals that are hooked into the company's electronic mail system. As noted earlier, Motorola is beginning to distribute the information on its MIRIS data base through its electronic mail system.

• *Comprehensive data.* A textual data base centralizes information, and allows senior management to get a better "big picture" view of the marketplace. Without such a data base, management must rely on disparate information sources often scattered throughout the company's various operating units.

The Disadvantages . . .

• *Inflexibility.* It becomes difficult and expensive to change the structure of a major textual data base. For a number of companies who have built textual data bases and have found their markets changing, restructuring has been extremely difficult to manage. The general rule of thumb is "The larger the system, the more difficult and more time-consuming the restructuring becomes."

• *Time and expense.* Data entry takes time and money. Large textual data bases, like Motorola's, require many hours and many keystrokes to enter and maintain the information. The software costs alone may be prohibitive for most companies, especially when this software package's sole application is for a competitor-intelligence data base.

• *Quality control.* Inaccurate, unscreened information can easily find its way into the system because of poor or nonexistent data entry guidelines. The larger the data base, the more you need to screen the information being entered.

• *Start-up difficulties.* Motorola believes that its MIRIS system would have had a far greater impact upon the organization if it had been able to make the data base available within one year. As it turned out, it took Motorola almost three years to make this system available to others outside the intelligence office. Motorola believes that to make a major system like MIRIS work, you need to bring it online inside of a year. In hindsight, they would recommend that others who are considering building such a mainframe-based system bring in outside software consultants with expertise in this area. These consultants would speed up the development and thereby allow the information to be loaded into the data base as soon as possible.

Guidelines for Success in Information Storage

"Having information is important," says David Heinzelman, manager of competitive evaluation at Xerox. "But if it doesn't influence what your company does, you're not doing your job." Heinzelman and his office live by this credo. Most of their competitor information is found in manual files, not on computer data bases. Although he has created small spreadsheets that are easy to update and maintain, Heinzelman and his evaluation team spend their time on evaluation, not on data entry. The result: Critical information reaches Xerox's management quickly.

Whether you choose to build a manual file or go electronic, or whether you use a combination of both, take note of the following guidelines:

• *Establish goals.* This is critical. Write down the goals you seek to achieve, and be specific. For example, "This data base will supply the sales force with the latest contract award announcements."

Spell out the goals at the beginning, for later on you will be accountable for the data base's success or failure. On the positive side, by clarifying the goals in advance, you have a far better chance of meeting them.

• *Identify user needs.* Determine in advance *who* will use the data base and *how* they will use it. Knowing the "who" will tell you the type of information you must collect; understanding the "how" will tell you the best way to organize the data base so that the user will get the most out of it.

• *Work within a realistic budget.* Build a data-base or manual-file system your monitoring program can afford. A big data base costs big money, both in its construction and in its maintenance. Most companies, as you will see below, will not—or cannot—spend the money Motorola has spent on its data-base system. If you cannot afford to hire the staff to input or analyze the data, as well as maintain the data base, take a different route. Turn to a manual file or a simpler data base. I have heard tales of woe coming from executives who have spent over $150,000 for software for their data base, then did not have the necessary staff to enter or analyze the information.

• *Make sure your storage system can deliver timely informa- tion.* Whether you choose a data base or a manual file to house your competitor data, make sure you can find the information quickly and with a minimum of effort. Your hard work gathering timely information will be wasted if you can't relocate that information in a timely manner.

• *Design a system that adds value to the information.* Your storage system should help you assess your competition. It should not just be- come an electronic notepad, a prettier way to write down the informa- tion. In the case of a data base, it should help you understand trends or anticipate a competitor's move in the marketplace. Even a manual file can pull two disparate pieces of information together to present a differ- ent competitive picture.

• *Identify existing data bases. Don't duplicate existing re- sources.* Because of the proliferation of microcomputers, executives throughout your organization may be creating their own private com- petitor data bases. Through your intelligence audit, try to find these data bases. A particular data base may not fit your needs to a tee, but it may save you hours of needless work, or may simply offer fresh information.

• *Organize information simply and appropriately.* Do not over- design the way you store information. By adhering to the lean-and-mean philosophy, you may find you have no need for a large textual data base. Throwing every bit of information into a system can only overburden it, cause programming problems, and limit access. The more data you en- ter, the more difficult the ability to access it.

• *Carefully select the information you are storing.* It is all too easy to pour scraps of paper into a file drawer, only to find a mess later on. When designing a manual file, ask yourself, "Are you collecting the most needed information? Can you find the information easily, quickly?"

• *Coordinate divisional files.* You may elect (or have been in- structed) to develop a decentralized file system. If so, attempt to coordi- nate the contents and design of your competitor files with those of other divisions. Lack of coordination means lost information. I will discuss coordination at length in a later chapter.

Looking at Data-Base Cost

There are a number of costs to consider when planning a data base. One note of caution, though: This is not a book on management information systems, or on how to run a data-processing office. If you are considering building a very large data base, I recommend that you contact your data-processing office or a reputable consultant for a comprehensive assessment of your data-base needs. These experts can outline the work flow necessary to design and maintain such a system.

The following list of expense categories comes from *Creating and Planning the Corporate Data Base System Project* (Leo J. Cohen, Prentice-Hall, 1983):

Data Conversion
- Transcription of data
- Keying in data
- Programming
- Machine time
- Clerical time
- Management time

Personnel
- Design
- Programming
- Clerical
- Machine time
- Management

Finishing Costs
- System testing
- Parallel operation
- Documentation
- Delivery

A Final Comment on Data Bases

Start out small. Avoid mainframes at the beginning of your monitoring effort. Besides, at the beginning, your energies should be focused on raising awareness, providing incentives, and collecting the information. It makes little sense to expend energy on a filing system unless you have data to store in it.

Resist the temptation to expand the manual file or computer data base immediately. I refer to Boyle's law in physics, which states that gas expands to fill the space available. Translating that into competitor-monitoring terms, it means, "The more you expand your filing system, the more information you will be tempted to store in it—whether or not that information is important." In turn, you and your staff will spend more time keying in the data than you spend collecting or communicating it. The result: The information is dated by the time it comes online.

While large textual data bases have their place, I favor the microcomputer and small data bases. The small data base forces the user to streamline his information and enter only pertinent data. The proof is in the pudding. I have seen at least a dozen competitor data bases that have truly added value to a monitoring program—and were even responsible for some direct marketing victories. These data bases were all contained on microcomputers. To date, I have seen only spotty results from mainframe-based competitor data bases, and few cases in which large data bases actually helped their companies achieve specific strategic or tactical victories in the marketplace.

CHAPTER 6

DELIVERING INTELLIGENCE:
Getting the Right Information to
Decision Makers

Delivering timely competitor information is the final, but critical, step in competitor monitoring.

To design the best communications system, you must consider who should receive the information and what communications vehicles are appropriate to meet that audience's need. In general, your audience is divided into two groups: the individual decision makers and the organization as a whole. The advertising industry labels these two types of audiences as "target markets" versus "mass market." Just as the advertising industry designs its messages to fit its markets, your monitoring program must deliver the right message in the right format to the right audience.

This section offers six effective and low-cost methods for delivering intelligence to the appropriate audiences. I have categorized these methods as either those designed for key decision makers or those intended for the overall organization.

FOR THE OVERALL ORGANIZATION

Newsletters

A concise, eye-catching newsletter is probably the best way to spread competitor intelligence throughout your company. For example, an in-house intelligence newsletter issued by a major health insurance company caused a great stir after only its first issue. The newsletter, which is reproduced in Monitoring Snapshot 16, inspired 15 managers to write or call with new information. And, according to its editor, the first few issues caused senior managers to question several marketing strategies.

This newsletter works because it is easy to read and filled with fresh information. The newsletter in Monitoring Snapshot 17 was not so successful. It was designed and published by the information center of a telecommunications company.

The newsletter in Snapshot 17 is hard to read and hard to understand. The vital intelligence is lost in the sea of text. Specific problems in this newsletter are:

• *It is too wordy.* It is hard for the reader to pull out the salient points.

• *Its format changes continually.* Sometimes the newsletter lists the information by company and other times by subject. This makes it hard for the reader to find the topic of interest.

• *The headings are centered.* They are difficult to see in the middle of the line.

• *There is nothing graphically appealing about the format.*

• *The one-page introduction to the newsletter is unnecessary.* The reader just wants to get down to the meat, the substance of the intelligence offered. The manager reading this newsletter does not care about "notations." The editor has to make it as easy as possible for the reader to find the information. The instructions should either be rewritten or eliminated altogether.

There are several ways to re-format the newsletter. One option is to organize the news by subject, as the writer of the Blue Cross newsletter did. A second option is to organize the information by company. Which-

MONITORING SNAPSHOT 16

A Newsletter That Stirred an Organization

This in-house newsletter, published by the marketing research department of Blue Cross/Blue Shield of Michigan, struck a responsive chord within the organization. After reading the first edition, 15 readers sent back new information that they thought the intelligence department should have. It also caused a senior manager to question the insurer's marketing position in a particular market area. What aspects of this newsletter's style and format do you find effective in communicating competitor information? (Note: Competitor's names have been disguised.)

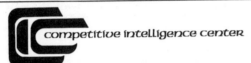

competitive intelligence center

DATE   JANUARY 1987   COMPETITIVE REVIEW   VOL. NO.   1.1

Welcome to the first issue of the <u>Competitive Review</u>. This newsletter is designed to help you stay current on national and local competitive intelligence.

Inside this premiere issue you'll find:

o   updates on the activities of several national competitors;
o   regional information on Michigan competitors; and
o   new entrants into the Michigan health insurance marketplace.

With a better understanding of our competitive environment, we believe you will be better equipped to face the challenges of your job.

<u>Competitive Review</u> will be sent to you each month. It is published by the Competitive Intelligence Center (CIC), a new segment of Market Planning and Administration. The information in it is gathered from sources within the corporation and gleaned from a variety of published materials.

We are excited about the opportunity to provide this service to you, and we look forward to your feedback and suggestions. We also encourage you to send any competitive news you can provide to the CIC.

Please send all intelligence information, questions, and feedback on the <u>Competitive Review</u> to:

****

NATIONAL REVIEW

COMMERCIAL COMPETITORS

Company A

o   Company A places hospital-bound patients in less costly settings through its Individual Case Management program. In 1985 the program involved more than 800 people and saved the insurer's customers more than $36 million. The program modifies the customary Company A insurance contract. Company A will cover the cost if the insurer, the physician, patient, family and employer all agree that an alternative setting is preferred over traditional hospitalization.

Blue Cross
Blue Shield

PREPARED BY THE MARKETING RESEARCH UNIT 225-8445 • MARKET PLANNING AND ADMINISTRATION

(continued)

Commercial Competitors - Continued

Company B

o   Company B is offering a triple option product through its subsidiaries. With
    the largest for profit HMO chain, Company B has about 900,000 enrollees in 17
    HMOs now and is shooting for 50 plans by 1988.

Company C

o   Company C is forming joint ventures with alternative providers to create new
    plans and market a triple option plan in 40 to 50 cities, projecting that
    50-60% of its insured population will be in either an HMO or PPO by 1990.

o   Company C purchased two HMOs and a PPO based in Phoenix, Arizona as part of its
    plans to offer a triple option choice in health care coverage.

Company D

o   Company D and its local partners including hospitals will invest $210 million
    over the next several years to start HMOs in most major metropolitan areas.

Company E

o   Company E launched its first PPO in June of 1985 and has since enrolled 100,000
    people in nine HMOs. An equal number of plans are about to come on-line.
    Ultimately, the company plans to build a nationwide PPO network.

Company F

o   Company F has 500,000 HMO enrollees in 19 cities.

o   Company F - experiencing slower growth with development of HMOs and alternative
    delivery systems; will have an organized delivery system in all of the top 90
    health care markets within three to five years.

****

MICHIGAN REVIEW

MICHIGAN COMPETITORS

Michigan-specific competition is divided into regions where the competitor has the
greatest activity. The regions will be further defined in the future as is
practicable.

MONITORING SNAPSHOT 16 (Continued)

Michigan Competitors - Continued

Company G

o   The Company G and Company H merger allows the two organizations to expand product lines.

o   Company G offers a PPO product through its licensed HMO.

o   Company G has a letter of "agreement" not a merger, with Hospital A to cooperate on mutual concerns.

o   Finally, Company G and Company I are negotiating the details of a joint venture.

Company J

o   Company J was purchased by Company K on December 1, 1986.

o   Company J wants to develop joint ventures with hospitals and has been contacted by four major hospital groups in the Detroit area and a physician group at Hospital B.

o   Hospital B decided in March that its clinics would no longer treat Company J patients who join the HMO after January 1, 1987. Hospital B owns 25% of Company L

o   Company J's goal is to increase membership 10-20% a year over the next five years.

Company M

o   Company M is affiliated with Company N and Company O. Company O is a joint venture of four hospitals. There are ten hospitals and over 1,400 provider physicians affiliated with this PPO.

Company P

o   Targets groups size 2 to 5,000 for its traditional health insurance.

o   Target areas to date have been Upper Peninsula, Grand Traverse area, Saginaw and scattered Mt. Pleasant area.

(continued)

NEW ENTRANTS

Company Q

o   Company Q

   Who: Offered by Company R
   Where: Detroit
   When: December, 1986
   What: A PPO which is part of a national network

o   Company S

   Who: Offered by Company T
   Where: Southeast Michigan
   When: Mid 1987
   What: A PPO; Company T currently operates PPOs in 4 U.S. cities and will
          start 19 more by the end of 1986.
   Why: "... because Company T local customers wanted the additional money
          savings that result from a PPO."
   How: Company T wants to sign up from 25% to 40% of the area's hospitals,
          then will recruit physicians with admitting privileges to those
          hosptials.

Next month in the Competitive Review: National information on hospital chains
will be provided along with third party business activity in Michigan and current
local competition highlights.

All references to competitive actions are based on generally available industry data
or trade releases.
/dld

MONITORING SNAPSHOT 16 (Continued)

We appreciate your comments as well as suggestions for future <u>Competitive Review</u> news. Please feel free to use the following space to provide the CIC with your competitive information and suggestions. We will accept competitive information in any form --- even phone calls.

- -

<u>COMPETITIVE INFORMATION</u>

DATE: _____

SUBMITTED BY: _____

PHONE: _____

MAIL CODE: _____

_____

_____

_____

_____

_____

_____

_____

_____

_____

_____

_____

_____

_____

_____

_____

_____

_____

Please send to: Competitive Information Center (CIC)

MONITORING SNAPSHOT 17

A Newsletter with Problems

This slightly disguised version of another in-house intelligence newsletter illustrates a number of problems. It lacks focus and is otherwise hard to read. What would you do to improve its appearance?

---

        (1)   Newsletter Sample
              (Source: Telecommunications Company)

August 15, 1985

MEMO TO: All Telecommunications District Managers and Above

SUBJECT: Newsletter

FROM: Jim Roberts, Information Center

     The enclosed newsletter is being circulated by the Infor-
mation Center to acquaint all managers with the products and new
ventures of telecommunications companies. It is composed of two
sections: "News" is arranged by topic and contains events of
interest in the industry. "New Products" contains new product
announcements arranged by product and company. Prices have been
included wherever available.   This newsletter is published
regularly, and covers the following product groups and subject
categories:

        Accessories
        Answer & Record Machines
        Cellular Phones
        Company News
        Computerphones
        Conferences
        Corded Residential Telephones
        Cordless Phones
        Do-It-Yourself
        Emergency Systems
        Intercoms & Pagers
        Feature Phones
        Modems
        Pay Phones
        Speakerphones
        Special Needs
        Telephone Systems

Three notations are used at the end of certain entries to further
assist readers. "Add. info. avail." indicates that the entry is
an abstract of a longer article. "Illus." indicates that an
illustration is available, and "RSC" followed by a number indicates the Reader Service Card number assigned to this entry by the
journal in which it first appeared. Frequently these numbers are
useful for obtaining further information about a product from the
manufacturer. No notation at the end of an entry confirms that no
further information was given by the original source.

Call me for further assistance.

(1) <u>Newsletter Sample</u>   (Continued)

<u>NEWS</u>

Cellular Phones

Bell Atlantic Mobile Systems and Budget Rent-a-Car of Philadelphia
are planning to put cellular mobile phones in 500 local rental
cars by the end of the year. Customers pay no additional fee for
rentals, but are billed $.90 a minute for usage of the phones.
Initial installation involves 200 intermediate, full-sized, and
luxury cars at seven Budget locations.
<u>Consumer Electronics</u>, June 1985, p. 168.

Computerphones

"Ten Year Market for Integrated Voice Data Terminals" is a report
which cautions that consumer buying patterns are shifting. These
shifts are likely to bring changes in vendor loyalty. The 106-
page report may be obtained for $1,950 from The Eastern Management
Group, Parsippany, NJ (201-267-3700).
<u>Telephone</u>, June 17, 1985, p. 134.

Company News

Mitsubishi Electric Corp. is planning to construct a multi-product
electronics plant in Braselton, GA., to manufacture cellular
telephones, computer display monitors, and other office automation
systems and projection TVs.
Add. info. avail.
<u>HFD</u>, June 17, 1985, p. 78.

Sony wasn't on the show floor at the June Consumer Electronics
Show but it has a new line of phones coming out soon. The company
is showing two integrated telephone answering machines in the $190
to $220 price range, and two clock radio/telephone combinations in
the $80 to $120 range in its private suite to selected customers.
Shipping is scheduled for the fall.
<u>Consumer Electronics</u>, June 1985, p. 168.

Conferences

"New Developments in Advertising, Marketing & Media Research," the
Advertising Research Foundation's 11th annual mid-year conference,
will be held at the Chicago Hyatt Regency on September 4-6, 1985.
Add. info. avail.

"Unixexpo," the Unix operating system exposition and conference
will be held in New York City September 18-20, 1985.
Add. info. avail.

ever option you choose, make sure it fits your readership's needs. In other words, are your readers more interested in the general subject areas, no matter who the competitor might be? Or are they unaware of who the new players are in the market? If so, they might prefer to see the company names highlighted rather than the subjects.

Here are a couple of ways you could have rewritten this newsletter:

Option One: Rewrite by Subject

TELECOM NEWSLETTER

What's New in . . .

Cellular Phones   Bell Atlantic Mobile Systems and Budget Rent-A-Car to put cellular mobile phones in 500 local rental cars by year's end. Customers pay only $.90/minute. (Consumer Electronics, June 1985, p. 168)

Computerphones   Consumer buying patterns are shifting toward Integrated Voice Data Terminals, according to a June 1985 study published by the Eastern Management Group, Parsippany, NJ.

Option Two: Rewrite by Company

TELECOM NEWSLETTER

What's New From . . .

Bell Atlantic . . . and Budget Rent-A-Car plan to place mobile phones in 500 local rental cars by year's end. Customers pay $.90/minute (Consumer Electronics, June 1985, p. 168).

Mitsubishi Electric planning to construct a multiproduct electronics plant in Braselton, GA, to manufacture cellular phones, computer display monitors, office automation systems, and projection TVs (HFD, June 17, 1985, p. 78).

Both of the above examples break out the information in ways that help highlight the vital intelligence. Without omitting information, this format and style can make a newsletter more readable. Why they work so well is explained on the following pages.

A Clear Newsletter . . . the Writes and the Wrongs

Eloquent writing takes talent. But clear business writing can be learned. Below are my tips for writing readable, attractive intelligence newsletters.

1. *Keep prose crisp.* A short, clearly worded newsletter is an effective newsletter. Use single-syllable words wherever possible. Keep sentences short. Avoid commas, semicolons, and colons.

By summarizing information, you can shorten your newsletter. Instead of transcribing an entire article, pull out the highlights. Then refer the reader to the appropriate file or article for more information.

2. *Use active, not passive verbs.* Active verbs convey an organization moving forward and willing to stand up for what it believes in. Passive verbs mask information and can lead to ambiguities and misinformation. So, stand up and be counted. (Oops! Should I have said "So, stand up and count yourself?") Use active verbs.

Some newsletter writers prefer to omit verbs altogether and write their text in staccato fashion. For example, instead of saying, "The product received rave reviews from a wide variety of professionals," you might say, "Product excellent, according to professionals. . . ."

3. *Use present tense, wherever possible.* Past tense makes the information sound dead and stale. You want your intelligence to appear fresh and current.

4. *Use bullets.* Bullets help draw the reader's attention to important information. Don't overuse bullets to the point that every item receives a bullet and, consequently, nothing appears important.

5. *Highlight strengths and weaknesses.* By describing a new product's strengths and weaknesses, you give the reader a more sophisticated knowledge of that new product. The reader then knows far more than if he had just read a straight trade-magazine article on the same subject.

6. *Restrict coverage to a handful of topics.* Don't become the Flying Dutchman, trying to go all around the map in one fell swoop. Restrict your newsletter to a half-dozen or so topics, and you will benefit from greater reader interest and readability.

7. *Use graphics to raise interest.* Anytime you can reproduce a photograph or a graphic of any kind and place it in your newsletter, you

will increase reader interest. In addition, use your department logo on the newsletter to make it distinct.

The computer company newsletter (Monitoring Snapshot 5) seen in an earlier chapter uses a spyglass to attract its readers' interest.

8. *Add color.* Black print on white paper can deaden interest. Some parts of your newsletter need color. While you shouldn't overdo it, adding spots of color can serve to highlight information and make your newsletter special and easy to spot in the in box. Here are some areas where you can use color to perk up your newsletter:

- Make your masthead a distinct color. I recommend blue or red.

- Print the newsletter on colored paper. Yellow works particularly well; it is the color of urgency, since telegrams, telexes, and other urgent messages often appear on yellow stock.

- Use color bars and colored lines to separate articles or to box in special sections.

In short, intelligence newsletters can:

- Provide your organization with regular updates on competitors' activities.

- Maintain awareness of the importance of competitor intelligence.

- Summarize major events occurring in your company and in the marketplace (for example, a report on a recently attended trade show).

- Call attention to any changes within your industry.

Displays

Take advantage of any opportunity to display competitor information. Displaying information is the best way to deliver messages about your competition to large groups of people.

Xerox has taken this credo to heart, as is evident from the following story reported in "Xerox World," the Xerox internal magazine (Winter 1983, page 8):

> From time to time, our competitive-evaluation people arrange special demonstrations of competitive products. Not long ago, they were displayed in the main cafeteria in Webster [NY]. Over a period of several

MONITORING SNAPSHOT 18

Newsletters That Communicate

These excerpts are from newsletters, published by marketing groups within Abbott Laboratories and a major brewery, which display competitor information clearly and concisely. (Note: in both cases only parts of the newsletters are used here.)

COMPETITIVE HIGHLIGHTS:
Abbott Laboratories: Diagnostic Division

FINANCIAL
AMERICAN MONITOR—Reported a profit of $2.6 million for its third fiscal quarter ended March 31, 1986. Of this total, $1.3 million was provided by operations of which $920,000 related to nonrecurring items. Sales for the quarter increased 33% from the quarter ended a year ago. The increase was a result of increased instrument sales in both domestic and foreign markets, and increased chemical sales.
Nexis
05/16/86

NEW VENTURES/MERGER AGREEMENTS
DIAGNOSTICS PASTEUR—Has signed agreements with BECKMAN INSTRUMENTS and SERONO DIAGNOSTICS to develop and market its products in the U.S. BECKMAN will use PASTEUR technology to develop DNA probes with non-RIA markers for diagnosis of bacterial and viral infections. SERONO subsidiary, ARES-SERONO, will market the French firm's MonAbrite range of MAB assays in all world markets except France and certain parts of Africa.
BBI
04/30/86

ELECTRO-NUCLEONICS—Announced that it has agreed to acquire distribution rights in the U.S. and Canada to PHARMACIA AB's allergy and other diagnostic product lines. In return for these rights, ENI will give PHARMACIA approximately $2.3 million in cash, in addition to 200,000 shares.Clinica
03/21/86

COLLABORATIVE RESEARCH—Will start marketing a pretest for cystic fibrosis within weeks through its Diagnostic Services Reference Laboratory. The test does not require government approval. Researchers found a second marker on the opposite side from the first marker on the gene. By being able to test for two markers that straddle the gene, researchers can be 99% sure whether the CF gene is present. The test will show whether a fetus 8–10 weeks old has CF.
WSJ
06/02/86

DUPONT—Introduced a new field flow fractionation (FFF) instrument at last month's Pittsburgh conference. It is called the model SF3-1000 and sells for $89,000.
Analytical Chemistry
04/86

(continued)

FUJI PHOTO FILM CO.—Has developed a dry-type multilayered film lab test system, capable of measuring sodium, potassium, and chlor, in a minute. Following the receipt of the Ministry of Health and Welfare's approval, the company will bring to market this summer the analyzer as "FUJI Drychem 800" and the slides as "FUJI Drychem slides Na-K-Cl". The newly developed system, which can use whole blood, is the world's smallest and light-weight portable type. It is expected to be of great use for emergency and on-the-spot testing.

Japan Pharmaceutical Letter
04/12/86

MOCHIDA PHARMACEUTICAL—Located in Tokyo, Japan, have developed a monoclonal antibody-based pregnancy testing kit which detects hcG and provides a result within two minutes. The company is awaiting permission from the Health and Welfare Ministry to market the test as an OTC product and expects the new test to supercede its other three pregnancy tests, which it claims, have a 75% market share in Japan.

Clinica
04/11/86

XYZ LABS—On Thursday, April 24, I overheard a group of XYZ sales reps engaged in a conversation regarding Strep A competition. The only information I was able to gather was that they had been instructed to offer their customers discounts of up to 20% off their current strep price in return for a contractual commitment in terms of an unspecified volume of purchases, and a guarantee to stick with XYZ for at least one year.

John Smith
04/24/86

ABC LABS—Has introduced B5's on the AD-2000. It requires no pretreatment and can process about 30 results per hour.

Susan Jones
CRME1
04/26/86

**BREWING INDUSTRY
INTELLIGENCE REPORT**

July 18, 1986

ANHEUSER-BUSCH

Anheuser-Busch Buying California Winery

Anheuser-Busch reached a preliminary agreement to buy the LaMont Winery of DiGiorgio, California, which is to produce Dewey Stevens Premium.

LaMont already produces Anheuser-Busch's Master Cellars draft wines. Terms of the sale were not announced.

"The winery currently produces our Masters Cellars draft wines, and will devote a greater percentage of its production capacity to meet the growth needs for that brand," said Michael Carpenter, VP of the Beverage Group.

The winery, which is on an 111-acre tract, has an annual capacity of 28 million gallons.

The winery has started to ship batches of Dewey Stevens, for packaging at outside bottling plants. Carpenter said Anheuser-Busch will build a packaging plant and warehouse facility adjacent to the winery to accommodate production of its wine cooler. The bottling lines should be in place by the spring.

St. Louis Post 7-12-86

Anheuser-Busch Enters Agreement for Water Rights

Anheuser-Busch announced July 14th that it had entered into a partnership agreement with Cabin Bar Ranch in which the brewery gets access rights to new water resources.

As part of the deal, Anheuser-Busch becomes majority owner of the newly formed Cabin Bar Association. Resources of Cabin Bar Ranch include "several natural springs of extraordinarily high-quality water", the brewery said.

"This agreement dovetails with our long-term business strategy of acquiring quality water sources coincidental with the Anheuser-Busch Beverage Group's increased activity in the bottled water market", said Michael Carpenter, VP of Beverage Group. "However, there are no plans for related new product developments at this time."

United Press International 7-14-86

Miller Does Not Mean to Insult Indian Tribe

Officials of the Miller Brewing Co. say it did not mean to insult Sioux Indian tribes by considering production of a new beer called "Dakota" which is another name for the Sioux.

"It is just a code name", said Alan G. Easton VP for Corporate Affairs. We are still in the research stage, and the name is one of several being researched as possibilities for the new beer brand", he said.

Associated Press 7-11-86

MONITORING SNAPSHOT 18 (Continued)

GENESEE BREWING CO.

Genesee Forms Leasing Company

Genesee Brewing Co. Inc. which announced earlier this year it would soon expand its business beyond beer, has formed a joint venture with another Rochester company. The brewery and Taylor-Bulane Associates Inc. formed Cheyenne Leasing Co. to broker equipment leases for large and medium size business for use as tax shelters. The new company will be headed by James F. Taylor, president of Taylor-Bulane since its formation in 1984.

United Press International 7-10-86

months, some 7,000 employees—in groups of 50 at a time—were given time off from their jobs to see what the competition had to offer.

A company can display competitor information in a number of ways, from a formal demo room to a simple bulletin board. While the above example describes a manufacturing firm's display, service firms can use this technique as well.

The Demo Room—Why and What Is It?

A demo (demonstration) room is simply a place where employees can review the competition's products. The best demo rooms allow employees to actually use these products in order to get a better feel for them.

A demo room can also speed up decision making. For example, a vice-president at a computer-hardware company had been receiving conflicting information about a competitor's new personal computer. He did not know which reports to believe. Hence, he could not make any marketing decisions to combat its entry into the marketplace. As soon as his company's evaluation group bought the new product, he headed downstairs to try it out. After seeing the machine in the flesh, speaking to the engineers who tested it, and pressing the buttons, he knew where he and his firm stood and he was able to act.

Demo rooms can work equally well for service firms. While you can't display machines, you can display product and price literature. You can place last year's brochures next to this year's for comparison. Next to each brochure, you could also post a fact sheet, describing the changes or improvements made from year to year. Since the literature is the physical expression of the service itself, a thorough examination of the literature can reveal how the service is promoted, constructed, and priced.

The Bulletin Board

The bulletin board is not only an excellent awareness-raiser, but it is also a great communicator of intelligence. The Xerox example in Chapter 3 clearly describes how quickly a display, such as a bulletin board, can convey timely information.

Communicating with Electronic Mail

Because electronic mail allows you to send messages to one individual or to thousands, it can be used as both a mass-market and a targeted communications tool.

Not unexpectedly, employees in high-tech companies like Digital Equipment and Hewlett-Packard communicate a great deal through electronic mail.

Ways to Communicate with Electronic Mail

The following are ways in which you can use your electronic mail system to communicate intelligence:

• *Storing competitor profiles.* You can create and store competitor profiles in a special file in your electronic mail system. At any time, a manager can sign onto that file and read the latest competitor profiles.

• *Exchange of information.* Use the electronic bulletin boards and conferencing features of your electronic mail system to exchange information with your company's experts. The "electronic bulletin board" is no more than a public file that everyone in the company has access to. Because it is a public forum, an electronic bulletin board can help you find the kind of expert you need. Usually these boards are categorized, so you need only look for the board of interest to you.

FOR KEY DECISION MAKERS

Reports

Memos and reports are such a common means of communication that many executives overlook the importance of making them clear, concise, and attractive. However, properly drafted memos and reports offer two very important benefits: One, your message can be very specific, and targeted to a small audience. The more direct the message, the more effective it is. Two, you can deliver the information almost immediately. Unlike a newsletter, you do not have to wait for a publication schedule to produce a memo.

What Makes a Report Attractive, Effective, and Sexy?

A real knockout of a report or a memo should cause its readers to stop and think. It should make them break their corporate stride and ask some solid questions about the competition.

Take a look at the following sample in Snapshot 19. This is an example of a powerful, one-page intelligence memo. It contains a lot of information in a short space. Notice the short sentences. Note, too, how the author uses asterisks to convey information. Snapshot 20, also below, is not quite so successful.

ANALYSIS OF SNAPSHOT 19

This memo is extremely attractive. It is short. Sentences are staccato, with active verbs. The memo presents the information by company name in alphabetical order.

The author keeps both text and numbers to a minimum. Each asterisk automatically tells the reader that other information on the company is available and to go back to the author for details which do not appear in the memo.

ANALYSIS OF SNAPSHOT 20

The opening page is long and wordy. The second page, though, is very clear, with short, taut sentences that convey hot competitor information in a flash.

I would cut the first page to a single short paragraph. The second page I would leave alone; it works perfectly as is. The matrix format is excellent. It guides the reader to the desired company and subject.

The report strikes a good balance between too much data and too little substance. By keeping the memo short, the author encourages the reader to ask for more information.

The report's author told me that these matrix memos have become so valuable at the company that managers maintain a file of them for future reference.

Reference Books

A competitor reference book is a binder containing a set of competitor profiles. The book is either stored in a central library, or copies are made

MONITORING SNAPSHOT 19

Short and Sweet Leaves

This newsletter keeps the news announcements short and leaves space around each news item, allowing each to stand out. This approach makes the newsletter very readable.

MANAGEMENT SERVICES/BUSINESS AND COMPETITIVE ANALYSIS
COMPETITIVE CONDITIONS OVERVIEW
July, 1985

(*) Denotes items reported in one or more publications

I. DOMESTIC BRANDS AND MANUFACTURERS

Acme   (*) Rumored to be extending its refrigerator vacation
                 an extra week to reduce inventory levels.

            (*) Will be marketing a line of dishwashers, sourced
                 from Farrell, by the end of the year.

Dawson   (*) Will lay off 200 hourly and 12 salaried workers,
                 effective August 1. Its planned move of room air
                 conditioners to Australia now seems to include
                 all of its room air line.

Dubham   (*) Introduced its 1986 room air conditioner line
                 early this year, claiming its units are smaller,
                 lighter, and retailing for less to compete with
                 offshore manufacturers.

Farrell   Rumored to be interested in the home computer
                 business and a possible related acquisition.

            (*) Approved its new three-year labor contract by 58%
                 of members; calling for an immediate one-time
                 payment equal to 1.5% of estimated annual wages,
                 a wage increase of 2% in June 1986 and June 1987,
                 and several job protection provisions.

            (*) Stated its second quarter earnings and revenues
                 for major appliances were "slightly ahead" of a
                 year earlier.

            (*) Will establish an Appliance Distribution Center
                 in Fresno, California.

                 Rumored to be interested in some Putnam and
                 Walker ovens, as its own supplier is apparently
                 unable to provide the volume needed.

116

MONITORING SNAPSHOT 20

Boxing in Financial Services

While the first page is weak and does not excite the eye, the second page of this memo is packed with information that is easy to pull out and easy to read. A different way to compose a memo, but one that works.

August 15, 198*

MEMO TO: Distribution

FROM: Intelligence Department

SUBJECT: Financial Services Industry Report: Mid-Month Update

Enclosed for your information is a new mid-month edition of Industry Report: Financial Services, prepared by the Intelligence Department. This update will consist of the matrix you are familiar with, organized by product line, showing activity by major competitors, as well as highlighting activities by other competitors.

Complete coverage of all items appearing in the mid-month issue will continue in the full Industry Report issue published the following month. If additional background is required on any information contained in this mid-month report, please let us know.

Significantly, the trend identified in the June Industry Report regarding increased activity by [Company] in international operations continues, with announced plans to increase corporate activities in France.

In addition, there has been a move by Japanese financial services firms to expand their international operations, reflecting the gradual financial deregulation now progressing in Japan. And as Japanese firms begin moving into international marketplaces, likewise foreign firms are beginning to gain access to the extremely attractive Japanese market which has long been subject to strict financial services regulation. Indeed, [Company] has been able to expand capabilities in Japan beyond its commercial banking activities into trust banking and securities: [Company] was one of nine recipients of Japanese trust banking licenses earlier this year, and the Ministry of Finance granted permission for [Company] to continue activities in the Japanese securities business even after its acquisition by [Company].

If you have any comments, questions, or suggestions regarding the new mid-month update report, please call.

(continued)

INDUSTRY REPORT: FINANCIAL SERVICES

Mid-month update

	Insurance	Payment Systems	Asset Management Brokerage	Banking/ Lending	Information Advisory Serv.
ProfitBank (PB)	•PB will become the biggest shareholder of municipal bond insurance firm in with possible future plans to acquire as much as 5%		•PB reorganized its institutional management units into a separate subsidiary in an effort to better serve specific needs of corp. clients	•PB announced plans to open branches in more than 10 cities in an effort to build up business with medium-sized high-growth companies.	•The PB/DB subsidiary has already installed its new multi-transaction switching and processing system in the Lo-Price supermarket chain.
U.S.-Express (USXS)			•USXS launched a $9 million national ad campaign focusing on its resources and personnel rather than on its USXS trademark.		
Mason Bank		•Mason will open its ATM statewide network by mid-January.		•Mason is running ads capitalizing on the Mason name to market mortgages. •Mason is negotiating to acquire a controlling interest in certain trading operations of General Mulch, a Georgia-based general trading company.	
Small Finance Inc.		•Small will lay off 300 employees and close its Washington government affairs office to cut operating costs. •Small's fast growing ATM network in Georgia recently merged with the Main Atlanta bank network.			
FastFinance, Inc. (FF)		•FF announced the first five banks to participate in its at home banking pilot.			•FF cut prices for electronic authorization services and offers rebates on members' monthly bills.
Ohio Holding (OH)	•OH is organizing a new insurance sub. to provide business liability insurance for 15 industrial firms.	•The OH consortium of banks will introduce an OH travelers cheque.	•OH filed applications with Fed. Reserve Bd. to form a trust bank; this is the first firm	•The OH bank sub. is cutting jobs from its worldwid workforce to control overhead expenses.	•OH will buy into FFR financial info network. •OH will acquire a 45% stake in $-Station, Inc. treasury workstation software producer.

and distributed to a handful of key managers. It is an excellent way to communicate a common body of information on the competition to your decision makers.

Besides providing a common base, competitor reference books are particularly valuable communications tools because they are:

• *Inexpensive to produce.* You need only a word processor and a copy machine. The reference book needs no fancy index or binder. The loose-leaf format allows for easy and inexpensive replacement of pages.

• *Easy to update.* Every time you change or add a competitor file, just make a copy and send it to the appropriate party for insertion into the book.

• *Easy to use.* Finding a piece of information in a competitor reference book is as easy as finding the company profile and leafing through a few pages. This makes it far more user-friendly than most automated competitor data bases.

• *Handy for networking.* Each profile should contain the analyst's name. This signature will increase the visibility of the research organization and help intelligence users know where they can go for further information.

Tips for Writing an Effective Reference Book

Reference-book formats can vary widely. The guidelines I offer below are based on successful reference books. As you read through the guidelines, see how they compare to the one-page reference-book sample on the following page.

• *Ensure ease of use.* Place reports in three-hole binders for easy replacement and removal.

• *Use a consistent format.* Use a consistent format for each competitor. The reader should know what to expect on each page.

• *Leave white space.* Allow enough white space and wide margins to make reading easy and to leave room for notes.

• *Place vital statistics at the top.* Place competitors' vital statistics, sales, profits, product lines, and other data in a box near the top of the page. This serves to highlight the most important data and trends.

Placing the hot information in a box is not a new technique for busi-

MONITORING SNAPSHOT 21

A Profile with Punch

This reference-book profile succeeds because it summarizes much of the important data on the first page. The boxed-in area permits the hurried reader to absorb quickly most of the competitor's vital statistics. This is a disguised report from a company's actual reference book.

Acme Printing Ink Co. -- Corporate Overview   Revised May 198*

```
FINANCIAL FY 12/8*    % OF REVENUE              PRODUCTS

Revenues $3.2M        Inks             73%      Inks yes
                      Machine Tools    14%      Machine Tools yes
Net Income   $.5M     Press Supplies   13%      Printing Presses no
                                                Press Supplies yes
                                                Wipes no
                                                Photoproc. Equip. no
```

On January 1, 198*, Acme launched a new line of machine tools, which have been extremely well received, and have overtaken press supplies as a portion of sales. Acme's resources (assets of $4 million, approximately 320 employees, shareholder equity of $900,000, and long-term debt of only $500,000) make it a solid force in the market, and could position it for introduction of yet another line of products. However, Acme is known as a conservative company, reluctant to make extensive changes without a firm cushion of financial reserve. The company's R&D effort has a budget of $400,000.

Sales apart from the new line were disappointing in 198*. The company has been making a strong effort to reduce costs in marketing, sales and general/administrative areas. In 198*, it will continue to give special attention to reducing staff functions and overhead expenses.

Acme has outlined some of its financial objectives for the next few years. It plans to reduce its current debt ratio (D/D+E). The company is looking for a return of 25%-30% on equity, and will try to recover more of its investment in the machine tools line as soon as possible.

Printing inks continue to be the mainstay of the company, and little change is expected in this emphasis. Inks generated $2.336 million of the company's 198* revenue, and over half of its net income.

ness reports. *Standard & Poors* and *Value Line* corporate reports place company highlights in a box at the head of each capsule company report.

• *Use illustrations.* Include charts and graphs where appropriate. Any time you can spice up your black-and-white pages with some graphic images, you will improve readability. Appropriate graphics will draw the reader's eye to the information that is most important.

News Articles and Clippings

People believe news articles. Wherever possible, use them to deliver competitor information to individual managers.

A newspaper article, in comparison with most internal company memos, will carry far more weight and be believed by many more people, even if both the memo and the newspaper article told exactly the same story.

One chemical company executive I interviewed carried this idea to an extreme.

"For weeks," he told me, "I had been trying to tell management that it needed to act on a certain competitive issue. No one paid much attention to my concerns.

"Finally, I just picked up the phone and called one of the national business papers and leaked a small portion of this information to a reporter. An article appeared the next day, describing the details I had passed along the day before.

"Wouldn't you know it," he chuckled, "my managers came to me all excited and declaring that we had to do something fast, or we might be in big trouble. They believed the article, and not me."

While this manager went on to say that he would not recommend that anyone else take up this practice, this story certainly illustrates the power of the typeset page.

Executives have explained a news article's credibility as a combination of two factors: First, because an article is typeset, and perhaps accompanied by a photograph, it looks official and accurate (far more so than an internally produced, typewritten memo). Second, since the article was written by an outside "expert," the information has an aura of truth.

Tips for Effectively Using News Articles

• *Send them when news breaks.* Periodically circulate a collection of news articles about your competition. Original clippings from newspapers or magazines are usually better than the printed output from a data-base search.

• *Attach articles to reports.* Attach articles to memos and reports to help give credence to the reports and help capture the executive's attention.

LOOKING BACK AT COMMUNICATING . . .

Speed and accuracy are crucial in the communications segment of competitor monitoring, just as they are in the other segments (i.e., raising awareness, organizing information). Whatever communications tools you use, they must fulfill these criteria. If they don't, you haven't yet found the right tools for the job.

CHAPTER 7

YOUR LIBRARY:
An Intelligence Goldmine

A well-stocked, well-staffed corporate library is vital for a successful monitoring program. The library is an ideal place to store competitor information because it is often centrally located and staffed by professionals who are expert at both organizing and retrieving information. Knowledgeable librarians can also save you countless hours researching outside sources.

If your company already has a library, this chapter will show you how to use it more effectively for competitor monitoring. If you don't have a library, this chapter will describe the basic materials you need to start one.

WHAT THE IDEAL INTELLIGENCE LIBRARY SHOULD HAVE

The Library Rule: The best corporate libraries provide a few key sources and then refer researchers to the rest; they do not try to provide all the sources themselves. Corporate libraries invariably have limited budgets, and will squander time, money, and energy if they try to emulate the Library of Congress.

In particular, your library should contain industry directories and specialty magazines, and have access to many data bases. The collection should focus on your company's particular markets. Should you occasionally need sources that your library doesn't have, you can always use a local public or university library.

Below is a brief list of recommended sources for your monitoring library. For a detailed review of sources, I refer you to my earlier work *Competitor Intelligence: How To Get It—How To Use It* (Wiley, 1985).

General Reference Books

• *Atlas.* Whether your-target markets are regional, national, or international, it always pays to have an accurate map available. Maps can tell you where a company's most likely suppliers, distributors, or even customers are located, and they are essential for planning a research trip to unfamiliar cities. A good atlas will also offer population statistics for towns and cities.

• *Corporate Directories.* Corporate directories are vital for quickly locating a company's addresses and for understanding subsidiary-parent company relationships. They also provide some "ballpark" financial figures (although you should verify those figures before using them for important analyses). *Standard & Poor's Register of Corporations* (McGraw-Hill) and Dun & Bradstreet's *Million Dollar Directory* (Dun's Marketing Services) list tens of thousands of companies and their subsidiaries. Included in each listing is the name and address, estimates of company sales, stock exchange listing (if any), product or service lines, primary bank, and law firm.

• *Directory of Directories* (Gale Research Company). This is a superb resource for finding industry experts. It lists thousands of directories in scores of industries, including buyers' guides, distributors' catalogs, and industrial directories. The coverage is international. The entries are indexed by subject and title. The publisher's name, address, and the sale price are listed for each directory. The book costs $125, but is well worth every penny. My staff and I have used the *Directory of Directories* countless times to dig out esoteric buyers' guides in obscure industries. As Karl Malden might say: "Don't leave your library without it!"

• *Directory of Wall Street Research* (Nelson Publications).   The best single book for locating Wall Street analysts. This directory lists Wall Street analysts by the companies they track (over 3,500 U.S. and Canadian companies are listed in this text), as well as by the industries they generally follow.

• *Encyclopedia of Associations* (Gale Research Company).   If there is an industry, there is probably an association somewhere representing it. This work is essentially a five-volume index to associations across the United States. If an association for left-handed veterans of a particular battle in World War II exists, this is the book that would have it. Some associations are no more than desk-drawer operations. In other cases, though—and this is where your ears should prick up—associations are repositories of vast pools of industry data. Some publish overviews of their industries and membership directories, and also compile statistics.

• *The IMS Ayer Directory of Publications* (IMS Press).   This directory indexes magazines and newspapers by their city of publication. It is an invaluable way to find local intelligence sources. The cost for this annual is approximately $95.

• *Industrial Outlook Handbook* (Government Printing Office).   For its sale price of approximately $15, you will receive brief analyses of 350 industries. While most of the reports discuss overall market conditions and growth, some, such as the one on the CAD/CAM market, list company names and marketshares.

The handbook also lists, at the end of each analysis, the sources from which the information was derived. You can then call the consulting firms, magazines, associations, or even other government agencies for more detail. The analyst who authored the report is also mentioned.

• *Standard Periodical Directory* (Oxbridge Communications). This directory lists thousands of specialty magazines, including many esoteric industry publications. The magazines are listed alphabetically by subject area. It costs over $300, but is well worth the price. Oxbridge also publishes a companion volume listing thousands of newsletters.

• *Statistical Abstract of the United States* (Government Printing Office).   If you ever need to find industrial or demographic statistics or the government office which compiles them, this is the book to go to. This text, hundreds of pages long and about the size of an almanac, includes summary data on the U.S. economy, exports and imports, shifts in the labor force, and population characteristics for all 50 states. It is a valuable and inexpensive source for every corporate library.

• *Thomas Register* (Thomas Publishing).   This is a 17-volume work listing almost every U.S. manufacturer by the product or products manufactured. It is the most comprehensive reference text on U.S. manufacturers. In addition to the product listings, it also has a section on the trade names under which companies sell. Six of the seventeen volumes are dedicated to reproductions of product catalogs for many of the companies.

• *Yellow Pages.*   Because they can supply you with names of local distributors, suppliers, manufacturers, and competitors, the Yellow Pages are a superb monitoring tool. The Yellow Pages display ads can be a godsend when you need to locate all of a competitor's locations, marketing strategy, or brands carried. For approximately $10 per hardcopy volume they give you a lot of bang for the buck. Their major drawback is their bulk. Fifty volumes can take up an entire bookcase. Many corporate libraries are squeezed into tiny spaces as it is, and cannot afford to make room for these massive tomes. There are a few online data-base alternatives, including the Electronic Yellow Pages available on the Dialog system (see Chapter 2).

• *World Almanac.*   There are many publishers of this paperback book of numbers, dates, and statistics of all kinds. It offers the intelligence gatherer a quick set of census statistics, summaries of U.S. government labor and trade information, biographies on famous persons, and maps of the world.

Periodical Indexes

While a commercial data base may provide you with a more current list of articles, a printed index can give you similar information less expensively. I recommend that most business libraries subscribe to the two following indexes:

• *Business Periodicals Index* (H. W. Wilson).   This index lists articles appearing in 300 business and management journals. It is easy to review and is a good source for overview articles on a company or on an industry. At less than $200 per year it should be within the budget of all but the smallest libraries.

• *Predicasts F&S Index* (Predicasts). The Predicasts organization offers both hardcopy and online versions of its U.S. and international periodical indexes. Each is sold separately. F&S reviews far more magazines than does the *Business Periodicals Index,* and it indexes all the articles by a seven-digit industrial code. Both the U.S. and international F&S indexes also offer a separate company index, listing the articles by company. F&S indexes are more expensive than their Wilson counterpart. An annual subscription to either the U.S. or international version costs $750, but in addition to the more extensive coverage, the extra money buys you more frequent updates. F&S sends weekly update sheets, whereas Wilson sends monthly compilations.

Industry-Specific Sources

For the following industry-specific categories, I refer you to the discussion in Chapter 2, "10 Easy Ways To Monitor Your Competition":

• Public filings
• Brokerage house reports
• Buyers' guides
• Trade-show directories
• Industry magazines
• Product literature and catalogs

BUILDING A MONITORING LIBRARY ON A BUDGET

Your corporate library need not be expensive. Nor do you have to acquire every single reference source. Just be sure that managers and librarians have access to vital sources—whether or not those sources are physically housed on your own library shelves.

If you follow the guidelines below, you can assemble an effective library for far fewer dollars than you might otherwise have thought:

1. **Don't buy what you can easily get for free.**

2. **Don't duplicate sources that you can easily borrow from somewhere else.**

With these guidelines in mind, you can build a low-cost, efficient monitoring library. Some specific suggestions:

• *Use your local public library.*   If you need a source only once or twice year, why purchase it? Often a telephone call to a local public library's reference librarian will answer your question. Reference sources are notoriously expensive. For example, a 500-page novel may cost you $20 in the local bookstore. A reference book of the same length could run $500.

• *Find the original information source.*   Many reference books rehash government literature or other free information sources. By going to the original sources, you can sometimes save a bundle. For example, instead of spending a lot for a report that contains an analysis of census data, you can get the raw data far less expensively through a number of commercially available data bases. A restaurant chain wanting to assess a competitor's site selection strategy may turn to a census data base; or, it could simply open a U.S. Census Bureau publication for much the same information at a far lower cost.

• *Look for online equivalents.*   An increasing number of expensive reference books are being made available online through commercial data bases. An example is the series of *Moody's Industrial Directories.* Most of the information from these reference books, which if purchased in hardbound book form would run you $1,000 or more, can now be found on the Dialog data-base system. On Dialog you pay for a Moody's search only when you conduct that search. Even if you use Moody's 20 times each year, you are probably better off using the data base.

• *Buy used.*   When you do not need the most up-to-date directory, try to find an earlier version of the desired text. You may save hundreds or thousands of dollars in the process. A number of years ago, I needed 10 years of annual report data available at my fingertips. There was no inexpensive data base that served my needs at that time. I turned to a book search firm, which I found through my local Yellow Pages and asked them to hunt down 10 years worth of *Moody's Industrial Directories*. The firm found them for me. A library had closed and sold off its entire collection to them. The total cost to me was less than $900. The total cost to purchase these books new would have been almost $10,000.

• *Contact university libraries for discards.* Ask the acquisitions department at your local business school library to notify you when they are discarding parts of their collection. They may have a schedule, or else they can take your request and call you at the appropriate time. I have found some real gems at no charge on the discard table at a local business school library.

• *Tap industry associations.* Industry or professional associations will often make a great deal of information available to you at no charge. You may be able to receive, gratis, the latest market study conducted on your industry.

In addition, your industry association may already have an excellent library. Use their experience with industry sources to help you pare down your collection. A one-hour conversation with the association's librarian will help you evaluate many of the sources you are considering for your collection.

• *Use interlibrary loans.* Special Libraries Association (SLA), an organization made up of corporate and academic libraries across the United States, has formed a network to swap information. Some, as in the Boston area, for example, have formalized interlibrary-loan systems. Should a member library not have a book or magazine, the librarian can check the Boston SLA Chapter Serials Directory to find out who does. The librarian can then call up the library with the source and place an order for an interlibrary loan.

A LIBRARY'S COMPETITOR-MONITORING SERVICES

Your company's library can perform numerous monitoring services for you. Librarians are trained to organize data efficiently and accurately.

Therefore, it makes sense that they are also the best qualified to access this data when it is called for.

Here are some of the competitor-monitoring services you should use your library for:

1. *Data-base searching.* To search data bases efficiently and accurately, you need a person who is expert in this area and who uses the data bases frequently enough to stay expert. The ideal person is a librarian who makes information gathering his or her full-time responsibility. Corporate planners or product-line managers can search data bases, but they may not search efficiently and may miss important information.

2. *Intelligence packaging and reporting services.* Because of their knowledge of printed and electronic information sources, librarians can efficiently select and package the information requested. Some corporate libraries have identified this need for more packaged, customized summaries and offer reporting services to their executives.

The Kraft Corporate Marketing Information Center (CMIC), for example, offers such services to its executives. A CMIC manager reports:

> "We put together monthly reports for each of several different projects. We begin each project with a global search, then review the search strategy each month. The monthly review allows us to change our reports as the client's needs change.
>
> "Each report contains not only the data base search results, but also information from our files and other recent research. This customized approach is particularly effective for our clients in the new product area, which is fast moving."

3. *Maintaining competitor files.* Sounds boring, heh? Possibly. A job few want? Maybe. But is it important? You bet.

Librarians are taught cataloguing and organizing of disparate documents—from books and magazines to product literature. What better place to house your competitor files than in the library?

The library is the best spot for your competitor files for a number of other reasons:

First, it is usually less affected by corporate politics. As such, others around the company may feel less hesitant contributing to the library than to, say, strategic planning, a department strongly resented in some companies.

Second, centralizing files at the library allows "one-stop shopping" for all information available on a competitor. At the researcher's request, a librarian can pull all the information from the competitor files, conduct a data-base search, scan the shelves for appropriate periodicals and reference books, and even offer a list of other contacts within your company who may be helpful. If the researcher needs to contract with an outside document-retrieval or research firm, the library can again steer him in the right direction.

4. *Publishing an intelligence newsletter.* Because librarians have access to a great deal of market and competitor information, they can often publish excellent newsletters. Many libraries have, as a result, decided to publish bimonthly, or monthly, newsletters. Sometimes the newsletters are no more than article summaries; other times, they contain more detailed descriptions of material that the library has included in the competitor files. Newsletter writing and publishing are discussed in detail in Chapter 6 of this book.

5. *Creating a clearinghouse.* For a number of companies, the library has created a master archive for all market studies and reports. Such an archive can save a company countless dollars in duplicate purchases.

The Kraft CMIC group has created an in-house data base called RECAP (Research Capsules) that has fully indexed millions of dollars worth of research purchased or produced for the Kraft organization. RECAP is extremely flexible and allows the user to search for a report by analyst, code word, title, date, or even the purpose of the research. For the first time Kraft has a handle on the market research that was becoming buried in its organization.

INCREASING THE INTELLIGENCE BASE BY TYING LIBRARIES TOGETHER

If you work for a large corporation, you probably have more than one library or information center. If that is the case, you must encourage them to share resources and expertise.

MONITORING SNAPSHOT 22

RECAPping Marketing Studies

This is a sample of Kraft's RECAP data base, containing millions of dollars of market studies which Kraft has purchased in recent years.

```
ACCESSION NUMBER : 983 8701
UPDATE DATE : 8701
DATE INITIATED : 840117
BUSINESS UNIT : NEW PRODUCT DEPT.
CATEGORY : NEW PRODUCT DEVEL.
BRAND/GROUP : GOOD PRODUCT
PROJECT TYPES : NEW PRODUCT DEVELOPMENT - CONCEPT/TASTE TEST
PRIMARY RESEARCH PURPOSE : NEW PRODUCT - NOT CONNECTED
                          WITH ESTABLISHED BRAND NAME
PRIMARY RESEARCH TYPE : CONCEPT TESTING -EVALUATION
PRIMARY COLLECTION METHOD : CENTRAL LOCATION TEST
ANALYSTS : DOE, JANE
SUPPLIER NAMES : JONES RESEARCH
TITLE : Three GOOD PRODUCT Taste Tests: Revised Flavor #1, Flavor #2
and Flavor #3.
FULL TEXT LOCATION : On Fiche by MRD No.
```

BACKGROUND
Marketing wishes to determine whether the revised formulas of GOOD
PRODUCT Flavor #1, Flavor #2 and Flavor #3 will result in a consumer
preference over the original formulas. The product formulas included
in this test have all demonstrated equal degrees of liking vs. a
competitive flavor in Sensory testing. Flavor #2 and Flavor #3 recipes
developed in the Cook's Program were preferred vs. current production. To
date, in-market performance has shown GOOD PRODUCT'S depth of repeat
purchasing insufficient to meet corporate objectives. In that repeat is
fostered by consumer satisfaction, product performance is a critical
ingredient to future brand success.

OBJECTIVES
The objectives of this study are as follows:
To determine whether consumers have a preference for the revised vs.
the original GOOD PRODUCT recipes.
To understand reasons for differences in preference; and.
To provide direction for reformulation of the revised recipes should
preference be marginal or in favor of the original formulation.

METHODOLOGY
Respondents will be interviewed in four geographically dispersed
cities. Pre-screening by phone allows for efficiency interviewing
respondents at 20 to 25 minute intervals and assures quality product
delivery. Nine hundred respondents (900) will be interviewed (300
per flavor).
Respondents will be shown both product formulas, with the respective
rice or noodle carrier. All product will be served unbrand, using
only an alpha-numeric code for the identifier. They will rate the
overall appearance of both. They will next taste each product and
be asked preference and reasons for preference. Order of tasting
will be rotated so half taste the revised (Cook's Program) recipe
first and half tast the current recipe first.
At this point, the current product will be removed. Each respondent
will be asked to rate only the revised recipe on 15 attributes. The
respondent will be told to complete the attribute ratings, regardless
of the preference they expressed earlier. Responses will be evaluated
by product preferred so as to provide more detailed direction for
reformulation, should it be necessary. Lastly, demographics will be
collected.
The sample size and methodology provides for 90 percent confidence
of a real difference should preference split as closely as 55:45.

DECISION CRITERIA
Consumer preference for the revised GOOD PRODUCT recipes over the
original product is required.
POPULATION
Respondents will be screened by telephone on the following criteria:
female heads of household, aged 21-64.
Use convenience main dishes (canned, frozen, and dry packaged).
Express definite:probable or tentative (might or might not buy)
interest in the GOOD PRODUCT concept.
Express interest in one or more of the test flavors.
LOCATION
Charleston SC.
Denver CO.
Chicago IL.
Sacramento CA.
CONCLUSIONS
Overall, all three revised GOOD PRODUCT items tested represent
substantial improvements over the respective original formulations.
In each instance, the revised product is preferred over the original
by a significant margin -- 59 percent versus 41 percent for Flavor #3,
71 percent versus 29 percent for Flavor #2, and 57 percent versus 43
percent for Flavor # 1. In terms of overall appearance, each of the
revised products is rated excellent:very good by 9 in 10 women. For
Flavor #3 and Flavor #2, this represents a significant improvement over
the original formulation. All three revised products receive
considerably better scores than seen in the original study on texture
of meat (less tough) and moistness of meat (less dry). All three also
fared better in terms of amount of sauce (less) and consistency of
sauce (not as thick).
RECOMMENDATIONS
We suggest that, prior to marketplace entry, the revised Flavor #3 and
Flavor #1 recipes be further refined according to the direction
received in this study and then submitted for a quantifiable taste test
versus competition.
TAXONOMIC CODES
#AQB #AQZ #A4N #BM #CA #CB #CD #DBA
TAXONOMIC DESCRIPTORS (TD):
ENTREES
SHELF STABLE PREPARED / SEMIPREPARED PRODUCTS
FLAVOR CHARACTERISTICS
NEW PRODUCT DEVELOPMENT
PRODUCT FORMULATION
PRODUCT TESTING
CONSUMER SATISFACTION / DISSATISFACTION

(continued)

SAMPLE ABSTRACT

PROJECT NO: 85225

COMPANY DIVISION: FROZEN FOOD

CATEGORY: SAUCES

PROJECT TYPE: ATTITUDE & USAGE, NEW PRODUCT DEVELOPMENT

QCODE: QUALITATIVE - FOCUS GROUPS

PROJECT CODE WORD: ZONK

SUPPLIER: JONES RESEARCH

ANALYST: DOE, JANE

TITLE: PROJECT ZONK EXPLORATORY FOCUS GROUPS

FULL TEXT LOCATION: On Fiche by Project Number

BACKGROUND:
The Frozen Division has been evaluating frozen qumquates
since 1984.....

OBJECTIVES:
The objectives of this research is to........

METHODOLOGY:
Six focus groups will be conducted on.......

DECISION CRITERIA:
Information from this study will be considered acceptable
if the following conditions prevail......

POPULATION:
Aged 21-54 years......

LOCATION:
Chicago, IL, Los Angles, CA

CONCLUSIONS:
Frozen qumquates are not seen as a specific category...

RECOMMENDATIONS:
It is recommended that Project Zonk proceed with......

TAXONOMIC DESCRIPTORS:
  PREPARED/SEMIPREPARED FOODS
  VEGETABLES
  PACKAGED DINNERS
  FROZEN PREPARED/SEMIPREPARED PRODUCTS

Small satellite libraries often spring up, almost unnoticed, within a large corporation. Librarians in these satellite libraries often know of each other but have never forged a formal network. They operate under different budgets and under different executives. Thus, they may often duplicate resources, catalogs, personnel, and expertise. A well-run monitoring program cannot afford such waste and potential loss of vital information resources.

General Foods has attempted to coordinate its 15 libraries by forming a network called Infonet. Infonet, in existence since 1981, offers librarians a forum for exchange of information and ideas, and gives the libraries leverage within the organization.

Because of Infonet, the libraries began refining their specific skills and collections to suit their own clients. Whereas before 1981 the many libraries stored the same material, each now offers unique, exclusive collections.

The technical library, for example, specializes in patent searching. Thus, if General Food's Marketing Information Center has a request for a patent search, it sends the client to the technical library. On the other hand, the marketing library has developed its own new-products data base which is unique in the organization. This data base can quickly scan almost any food category and print out the latest information on new products.

This network has allowed General Foods for the first time to amass all its libraries' holdings into a single online catalog. By late 1987, General Foods employees will be able to search the total collection of an estimated one million-plus items, via terminal and modem, from anywhere in the company.

To maintain this network, Infonet has aggressively marketed its services and its libraries. It regularly collects a list of new hires from the personnel department. Each one of these new hires receives an invitation to a training program about the company's library network. Also, each new employee receives in his orientation packet a booklet describing Infonet. Infonet's librarians try to get their libraries mentioned in company newsletters and magazines and even try to receive some local press coverage in General Foods' home town of White Plains, New York.

If there is a lesson in all this, it is that pooling corporate library resources is, if not top priority, certainly important. The payoff can be a large dollar savings, as well as a smoothly running competitor-monitoring program.

A VIEW FROM THE STACKS

The corporate library serves many purposes. But as far as competitor monitoring is concerned, the corporate library is a critical part of the program. Its resources, personnel, and services make it an ideal place to store and maintain much of the information that typically gets lost throughout the rest of the organization. If your corporate library has been relegated to the backwaters of your company and not used often or taken very seriously, I recommend you give it a second look. You and your organization may be sitting on an intelligence gold mine.

CHAPTER 8

BUILDING AN INTELLIGENCE DEPARTMENT

For many intelligence gatherers, competitor monitoring is very much a part-time job. But as their companies' monitoring programs mature, others find themselves developing intelligence departments that include several full-time staff members. This chapter is specifically written for the managers of such departments, and will help you find and train intelligence analysts, develop budgets, and manage department operations. This chapter should also help intelligence analysts develop their own skills and better plan intelligence projects.

The three major issues covered in this chapter include:

1. *Hiring and training analysts.* This section discusses who to hire, how to find the right candidates and how to train staff.

2. *Controlling program costs.* This section illustrates techniques for tracking your expenses and keeping costs low.

3. *Making projects work.* This section will outline the ways you can best estimate deadlines and costs for various intelligence-gathering tasks.

THE INTELLIGENCE ANALYST

The intelligence analyst conducts interviews, assembles data from published sources, and prepares reports. He pulls the disparate pieces of competitor information together into a coherent whole.

Hiring Analysts

A good intelligence analyst should have the following characteristics:

• *Creativity.* The analyst must be a creative, resourceful individual who is not intimidated by requests to obtain difficult information. This person must be able to develop sound plans for gathering data, as well as alternative plans when problems arise.

• *Desire.* Few people really enjoy sleuthing for information. Yet, for an intelligence analyst, that determination to find the answer, much more than intellectual ability, is the key factor for success.

In addition, successful analysts are sticklers for detail. They are not satisfied with half-baked answers. If answers seem incomplete, good analysts will pursue questions until they are answered to the best of their ability.

• *Interviewing skills.* The analyst should have a pleasant voice, the patience to let interviewees ramble, the guts to ask tough questions, and skin thick enough to handle frequent rejection. The last skill is particularly important, because thin-skinned analysts develop phone-phobia and will use any excuse not to conduct interviews.

• *Writing skills.* While writing skills are less important than interviewing skills, you need an analyst who can produce readable copy. Unlike interviewing skills, which depend in part on the analyst's personality, basic writing skills can be taught to most analysts. Nevertheless, hiring an analyst who is a terrible writer can cause you headaches.

How Do You Find the Right Analyst?

You can interview potential analysts. You can even train them. But first you have to find them.

Finding the right candidate can be difficult and frustrating. Many of my firm's best analysts walked through my door by chance, not by de-

MONITORING SNAPSHOT 23

Opportunity To Be an Analyst

Becton-Dickinson has sought "opportunity analysts" to assess markets and the competition for its R&D group. As you can see from the description, competitor monitoring is only part of the job; the rest of the job involves more general market-research tasks.

© Becton-Dickinson. Reprinted with permission

POSITION DESCRIPTION

POSITION TITLE: ___Opportunity analyst___   **INCUMBENT:** _____

DEPARTMENT: _____ **LOCATION:** _____

DIVISION _____

GENERAL FUNCTION

Responsible for developing and analyzing assigned marketing intelligence and research activities. Plans, designs, and executes data-collection programs and projects for identifying new products or markets and changes to existing products or markets which directly affect the profitability of the assigned areas. Provides management with information for decision-making purposes, participates in planning functions, and in the development of marketing positions for new market and product opportunities, through systematic data collection, evaluation, storage, analysis, and reporting. Reports to the Group Manager, Immunodiagnostics.

RESPONSIBILITIES

1. Monitor and evaluate competitive position in defined marketplaces:
    A. Maintain up-to-date files on competitors and emerging competitors.
    B. Acquire and evaluate competitors' products in the assigned area.
    C. Develop and maintain informational files on new product submissions and market evaluation.

2. Identify opportunities in the assigned markets:
    A. Provide information on users of the company's products, including physicians in private practice, group-practice physicians and laboratory technology assistants. This includes periodic visits to physicians' labs and distributors to gain first-hand knowledge.
    B. Conduct primary research studies as required: includes determining appropriate methodology, questionnaire development, validation, coding, administration, tabulation, analysis, and written report of findings.
    C. Conduct secondary research studies as required; includes literature search, identification of secondary sources, validation of source material, written analysis, and report of finding.

(continued)

3. Establish and maintain a marketing data base for ongoing projects as assigned.
POSITION DESCRIPTION
Opportunity Analyst
Page 2

4. Establish effective intradivisional and interdepartmental relationships to maintain awareness of current issues and concerns.

POSITION REQUIREMENTS

1. Knowledge and Education
   A. Basic knowledge of marketing principles, especially those emphasized in the health care industry.
   B. A bachelor's degree in science or business; M.B.A. desirable.

2. Experience—A minimum of one year in health care market research and three years related experience in medical diagnostics.

ACCOUNTABILITY

1. Conducts market research studies within approved expense budget.

2. Responsible for meeting market research objectives for the timely education, or new-products and new markets; and for working within the operating budget of the department, as assigned.

Prepared by:_____   Approved by:_____
Date:_____   Date:_____
Incumbent:_____
Date:_____

sign. A case in point: A friend of mine had struck up a conversation with a future analyst while she was lying under a tree in the park. Wanting to ask her out on a date, he found out that she was between jobs and that she also had done a great deal of telemarketing and sales work. I don't know whether or not he ever did take her out on a date, but he did recommend her to me for an analyst's job I had open at the time. The match turned out to be a good one, and she became a successful researcher.

Such stories are good for the cocktail-party circuit, but bad for building an intelligence staff. You need more methodical ways to find analysts, both inside and outside your own company.

You can try placing an ad in the Sunday classifieds section of your local newspaper, but I have had only mediocre results with this approach. Usually, I have had to wade through two hundred responses to come up with, at best, three candidates. You may want to consider these other options:

1. *Use trade magazines.* These are the best sources for analysts who know something about your industry. While industry experience isn't essential for a beginning analyst, experienced analysts are more desirable because they can be trained more easily. In addition, they are more likely to stay in the job than an inexperienced person who doesn't really know whether he will like your industry.

2. *Advertise in advertising magazines.* I have found that the advertising industry trains excellent intelligence analysts. Advertising agencies use internal research to prepare for client presentations and ad campaigns. Analysts who survive in the fast-paced agency environment are usually creative and hard-working.

3. *Post notices at university placement services.* If you are looking for a sharp, energetic analyst, whom you are willing to educate about intelligence-gathering and about your industry, university placement services may be for you.

Place your ads in the university's individual schools. In the past I have posted notices in business schools, communications schools, and library schools. The response has been good. Many candidates have had little job experience, but some have been out in the business world for several years prior to their schooling.

4. *Hire from within.* The best source for analysts with direct industry experience is within your own company. The personnel office, or others in your firm, can direct you to possible candidates.

A major chemical company, when it began a monitoring program, pulled together its intelligence staff from among its own employees, some with 25 or more years of experience with the company. They brought with them loads of industry contacts and a certain savvy not evident in recent business school graduates. Their experience also gained them respect with senior management. This respect meant that senior management would give serious consideration to the competitor information they gathered.

5. *Ask your staff for referrals.* Some of the best candidates that have crossed my firm's threshold have come via referrals from my staff. Your staff knows best the demands and the challenges of the job and can help you find people that you can't reach through advertisement.

6. *Tap professional societies.* Circulate job advertisements through marketing, advertising, or other professional societies. For example, if you are in the banking business, you may want to contact a banking club or society for financial analysts. You can either place an ad in the society's bulletin, or you can find those of your company employees who are society members and have them network through the society.

Training the Troops

No matter how talented newly hired analysts may be, they probably need a good deal of training. Because there is no official degree or business-school course in intelligence gathering, most analysts learn sources and techniques on the job. Yet a good, solid training program can help the analyst up the intelligence learning curve a lot more quickly. Below is a "course outline" for an analyst training program.

"Competitor Monitoring 101"

• *Knowledge of secondary sources.* Before your analyst tears into data bases or conducts interviews, he should know what your corporate library contains.

Aside from exploring your company's library or libraries, the analyst should also visit any major business-school libraries located nearby. He should investigate the availability of the following sources and services:

- *Reference librarians and the services they offer*

- *The variety of Security and Exchange Commission Reports*

- *Competitor literature on file*

- *Technical literature on file*

- *Newspapers, magazines, and trade journals*

- *Interlibrary loans*

- *Corporate services provided by the library (e.g. special newsletters)*

- *Data-base training.* The analysts should receive official data-base training on at least a half-dozen of the major data-base systems. An analyst without knowledge of data bases is like an airplane pilot flying without the proper training. With luck, the analyst, like the pilot, may complete his mission; then again, he may not.

Data-base training is generally inexpensive (usually less than $150 for one or two days), and extremely informative. Below is a list of courses offered by Dialog, the leading data-base supplier:

System Seminar (for beginners)
    Beyond The Basics
    Business Seminar (data bases for business research)
    Chemical Information Seminar (chemical substance searching)
    Company Intelligence Seminar
    Humanities/Social Sciences Seminar
    Legal Applications Seminar (including trademark searching)
    Library Applications Seminar
    Medline Seminar (National Library of Medicine data base)
    Patents Seminar
    Science & Technology Seminar

For further information, contact:

Dialog
>3460 Hillview Avenue
>Palo Alto, CA 94304
>415-858-3785

Other data-base suppliers offering inexpensive training programs are:

BRS (Bibliographic Retrieval Service)
>1200 Route 7
>Latham, NY 12110
>518-783-1161

Dow Jones & Co., Inc.
>P.O. Box 300
>Princeton, NJ 08540
>800-257-5114

Newsnet
>945 Haverford Road
>Bryn Mawr, PA 19010
>800-345-1301

Nexis
>Mead Data Central
>P.O. Box 933
>Dayton, OH 45401
>513-859-1611

SDC (Systems Development Corporation)
>2500 Colorado Avenue
>Santa Monica, CA 90406
>213-820-4111

Vutext
>1211 Chestnut St.
>Philadelphia, PA 19107
>215-665-3300

If you feel that these sessions are either too expensive or inconveniently timed, you may be able to persuade the service firm to offer a seminar onsite at your company. You can also go the more spartan route and have your library staff present a data-base training session of their own design.

• *Writing.* There are two skills that the analysts in my company absolutely require of new recruits: They are *writing* and *interviewing.* If new analysts can't write, send them to one of the many seminars on business writing, or to an evening-school class at a local community college. There are many writing courses available to you.

• *Telephone interviewing.* If the analyst lacks previous interviewing or telemarketing experience, then he will probably need some training.

Before putting your new analysts on the phone from day one, you may want to sharpen their skills through a seminar. You will find that there are plenty of commercial seminars that teach a broad range of telephone skills.

Remember, a good deal of your intelligence will come to you via the telephone. If your analysts are inept on the phone, then you can dismiss any hope of receiving good, solid competitor data. In contrast, a superb telephone interviewer can elicit a gold mine of information by just asking for it in the right fashion. (For details on telephone techniques, I refer you to my earlier book *Competitor Intelligence: How To Get It—How To Use It,* Wiley, 1985.)

• *Financial analysis.* I have found that analysts who are good interviewers and writers often don't have a great deal of training in financial analysis. Nevertheless, your intelligence department may require these skills. There are many ways for an analyst to receive training in this area. The analyst can attend night school, be apprenticed to your strategic-planning department (or equivalent), or attend a seminar on the subject.

• *Technical training.* This is applicable for any company with a highly technical product or service to sell. Aside from reading the available lay literature on the subject, analysts should meet scientists in R&D and develop contacts who can help them with technical questions.

• *Sales.* Because the sales force is a prime source of intelligence, analysts should make every effort to get to know and understand the sales force and the information it collects. They should attend sales meetings and occasionally even accompany salespeople on their trips.

• *Spreadsheet packages.*   Electronic spreadsheet packages, such as Multiplan ® or Lotus 1-2-3 ® can be extremely useful when applied correctly. As Chapter 5 showed, they can be very helpful tools in organizing competitor data. The best way to learn how to use these packages is by taking the software tutorial often provided along with the spreadsheet program. You can also take one of the many commercial seminars available, but I recommend trying to figure it out yourself first.

Training by Assignment

During this training period, you can motivate the analyst by giving a specific assignment to be completed as each new skill is learned. For example, tell the analyst you would like to better understand Company X's distribution system, its cost of operations, personnel involved, past successes and falures, and so on. Then tell the analyst to investigate each of these aspects while going through the training phases. For example, when learning how to use the corporate library, the analyst can retrieve articles and other data relating to the assigned company and its distribution channels. During the telephone-training phase, the analyst can conduct interviews to obtain more timely information. The goal is to force the analyst to explore each newly learned skill in depth and through a "real-life" case.

CONTROLLING COSTS

Your company's monitoring program can continue to grow without necessarily adding a great deal to overhead. In this section, I present ways to keep costs down while you build your monitoring program. But first I want to debunk a couple of commonly held myths about big companies, big budgets, and any relationship these factors may have to successful monitoring programs. Here are my observations:

Myth 1: *Large monitoring staffs mean better intelligence.* Nothing could be further from the truth. I have found companies who, overnight, have built enormous staffs of intelligence analysts, only to find that they are gathering inadequate information, or that the computer system they built to serve the staff is actually controlling the staff. Whether you are a Fortune-500 company or a small corporation, you are always better off starting small.

Myth 2: *Large companies are better at tracking the competition because they have the resources.* Large companies wish this statement was true. Some companies have started their competitor-monitoring efforts without a firm plan, scattering and duplicating resources; this helter-skelter effort has hindered their success.

Small companies and their employees are often more attuned to monitoring the competition than are large corporations. In a small company, all employees, even the president and senior officers, know it is their job to keep tabs on competitors. This unity of purpose breeds heightened awareness and good intelligence. Large corporations tend to engender the feeling that the "other guy" is tracking the competitor. The result: No one may be doing a good job of watching competitive activity.

Three Ways to Keep Costs in Check

1. Delegate Responsibility

A successful monitoring program may find that it has become the belle of the ball in the sense that it receives more requests than it can handle. You may feel that the only alternative is to plead for more money to hire more staff. Instead, you should look for others within the organization to act as escape valves by helping to collect the raw intelligence. By continually extending your network of intelligence gatherers, you can at least pass on the intelligence-gathering responsibility to others, leaving the compilation and analysis of the information to your staff.

2. Charge Back Services and Expenses

Another way to stretch a squeezed monitoring budget is to do what other service departments have done: charge back your services and project expenses to your internal clients. Charge-back systems work best if your department performs a lot of custom research projects for other departments. But they do not work as well for ongoing monitoring programs. Before you consider a charge-back system, understand the potential harm you can do to your cause. You need the whole company's cooperation to establish a good monitoring program; unfortunately, if you charge for your services, other departments may not be so willing to contribute information. How you decide this issue will very much depend on your corporate culture. If your organization is one where every service group charges back for services rendered, then you may want to do the same. If your monitoring program would be the first to jump into these waters, you might be making a big mistake setting a fee-for-service charge.

3. Track Dollars with Timesheets

Whether or not you are charging back your costs, you need to track how your professional staff spends its time.

Your entire staff should fill out timesheets that account for the staff's project and nonproject time. The time sheets provide several benefits:

• By tracking the staff's hours over a period of time, you can justify requests for additional help.

• You can identify specific time drainers, or time wasters. If your timesheets tell you, for example, that your staff is spending considerable time searching through libraries, you may need to hire a librarian to free your analysts to do other work.

• By keeping historical records of time spent, you can better estimate the staff time needed on an upcoming project. These records will give you planning insight.

MAKING PROJECTS WORK

As you develop a large-scale monitoring program, you will probably start conducting specific, in-depth research projects on certain industries or companies. The more research projects you and your staff undertake, the more you will need to manage your time, deadlines, and costs for each project. In this section, I want to help you manage specific research projects.

Running a competitor research service is like running any other service business. You must try to meet your internal clients' needs each time you undertake a research assignment. All you need is a handful of failures to brand your monitoring program a loser.

By following the guidelines below, you will be able to save your staff wasted time, better anticipate project demands, assess clients' requests, and ultimately deliver intelligence that contributes to better management decisions.

Taking the Research Request

An analyst must know how to accurately assess the client's research needs. Here are the steps involved:

1. *Meet with the client before starting research.* The analyst should meet at least once with the person requesting the research. If he is not able to meet in person, the analyst should interview the client at length via telephone before beginning the assignment.

In this meeting the analyst should first establish a rapport with the client, and second, try to gather all the information the client has on the research subject. Unless the analyst asks for it, the client may never think to give certain data. A preliminary meeting between the client and the analyst can also be used to air problems and sort through questions.

2. *Define the request.* The analyst must be sure he understands the request. The analyst thus must ask the client six basic questions:

- Who asked for the information?
- What information do you need?
- When is your deadline?
- Where will you use the information?
- Why do you need the information?
- How do you want the information delivered?

In order to make this process as painless as possible, the analyst should prepare a questionnaire that asks these questions; but the analyst, not the client, should fill it out. The analyst should have the questionnaire in front of him when taking the request.

After the analyst has gone back to his office and pondered what was requested by the client, he should then write up the request as he understood it and show it to the client for approval. If possible, have the client sign the request. See the following page for the sample request form used by a manager at one major consumer products firm.

Repeat the request back to the client to insure clarity. The reason for this is twofold: to make sure you understand the client's intent and to make sure that the client understands what he or she said. Remember, not all of us listen to ourselves very well. Some of us even mouth words whose import we are not completely sure of.

3. *Understand decisions to be made.* During the initial meeting, have the client explain the decisions to be made based on the information, or the reason for the request. This explanation helps the researcher identify and gather additional valuable information that might go beyond the stated scope of the project.

4. *Keep in touch with the client.* The analyst should maintain contact with the client throughout the project. Because intelligence gathering is a fluid process, the client may change the original request as new information is received. Keep in mind that the client may have made the original request partly out of ignorance. Thus, the more information the analyst feeds the client, the more likely the request will change. Certain questions will become more important; other questions will fall by the wayside.

5. *Provide an interim report.* An interim report will force the analyst and the client to sit down and review the results. After reviewing the report, the client will then decide how much more information he needs and whether to change direction or end the project altogether.

6. *Follow up with a visit or a phone call.* At project's end, the analyst should visit with the client. The analyst's job at this meeting is both to ask questions and to listen. The analyst needs to see if the client was satisfied or whether a new approach might be needed in the future. The analyst should ask: Was the report useful? Were any parts of the study more useful than others? How will the information be used? Did the client find the report format easy to read? What suggestions might

MONITORING SNAPSHOT 24

Competitor-Monitoring Request Form

The manager who uses this form makes sure that his client signs each request. This procedure insures that the request was given, received, and understood.

(Source: Multinational Industrial Company)

STRATEGIC INFORMATION

STATEMENT OF INTENT

TITLE: _____   PROJECT NO: _____

GROUPS: _____   ROUTING: _____

LINE(S) OF BUSINESS: _____   _____

PROJECT ORIGINATOR: _____   _____

PROJECT MANAGER: _____   _____

NEEDED BY: _____   _____

HOURS TO COMPLETE: _____   _____

EXTERNAL COST: _____   _____

I. ISSUES/BUSINESS QUESTION ADDRESSED:

II. PROJECT OBJECTIVES:
  A. PRIMARY OBJECTIVE:

  B. SECONDARY OBJECTIVES:

(continued)

III. WHAT DECISION(S) COULD BE AFFECTED BY THIS PROJECT?

IV: PROJECT TEAM

NAME: _____   ORGANIZATION: _____

_____   _____

_____   _____

_____   _____

_____   _____

_____   _____

_____   _____

V. PROJECT TIME LINE

START DATE: _____

DESIGN COMPLETE: _____

EXECUTION/ANALYSIS COMPLETE: _____

MANAGEMENT REPORT/PRESENTATION: _____

DOCUMENTATION COMPLETE: _____

the client make to improve the reporting style or client-analyst relationship in the future?

Realistic Project Planning

Running helter-skelter into a research project without any forethought or planning can create terrible problems for you and for your client. On the other hand, good project planning will help you:

- Accurately judge a project's true delivery time.

- Keep costs down.

- Use your research sources wisely. You will not "blow" good sources by calling too soon or asking the wrong questions.

The following are the steps to take when planning a project:

Step 1: Break Down the Questions

Your department may receive research requests that contain several questions. The best way to anticipate the amount of work required for each project is to break down each question into the tasks needed to answer that question. You can then estimate the hours it will take to accomplish each task, and add those hours together to estimate the total project time.

An example of such an analysis follows:

Question 1: What territories does the company sell in?

Research Request	Time
• Review Yellow Pages listings	2 hours
• Literature search of local newspapers	5 hours
• Obtain company literature, annual report, etc.	1 hour
• Interview independent sales reps	15 hours
Subtotal:	23 hours

Question 2: Who does the company sell to?

Research Request	Time
• Locate and interview distributors	10 hours
• Locate and interview OEM's	5 hours
• Retrieve and review trade-magazine articles	5 hours
• Locate and interview store buyers	10 hours
Subtotal:	30 hours

Question 3: Who are its customers?

Research Request	Time
• Interview competitors	5 hours
• Review annual report	2 hours
• Review product literature	5 hours
• Locate and retrieve press releases	3 hours
• Locate and interview shipping companies	10 hours
Subtotal	25 hours

Question 4: What are its distribution channels?

Note: No additional time required for this question, since it can be answered using the research conducted for Questions 2 and 3 above.

Question 5: What markets does it hope to penetrate?

Research Request	Time
• Interview trade-magazine editors	5 hours
• Locate and interview Wall Street analysts in this field	5 hours
• Locate, retrieve, and review the latest analyses	5 hours
• Locate and interview customers regarding approach sales force has taken with them	10 hours
Subtotal:	25 hours

Question 6: Is the company a low-cost producer?

Research Request	Time
• Retrieve loan filings for equipment purchases	2 hours
• Contact machinery suppliers for automation level of plant	10 hours
• Examine union contracts	5 hours
• Retrieve and review town filings from tax assessors	5 hours
• Locate and interview major suppliers	10 hours
Subtotal:	32 hours

Question 7: What products does it plan to release in the next year?

Research Request	Time
• Review patent filings	10 hours
• Attend trade show and retrieve available product literature	10 hours
Subtotal:	20 hours

Question 8: Can the company afford to enter a price war?

Note: No additional time required for this question, since it can be answered using the research conducted for Question 6 above.

Question 9: What is the company's advertising strategy? Where will it advertise this coming year?

Research Request	Time
• Interview advertising directors for likely trade magazines	3 hours
• Review three years of historical data from Leading National Advertisers, a source of corporate advertising expenditures	5 hours
• Interview advertising account managers from former agency	2 hours
Subtotal:	10 hours
Grand Total:	165 hours

This translates into approximately four weeks of work, based on a 40-hour week. But since it is very difficult for an analyst to devote all his time to one project, you should budget five weeks.

You could cut the time involved by adding an extra analyst. But don't expect to pile a dozen individuals onto a project in hopes of finishing sooner. An analyst needs to get a feel for a project. Most projects are big enough for only one or two analysts to get this "feel." In addition, some research tasks simply take time, either in waiting for a package to arrive or for returned phone calls. Also, it takes researchers time to assimilate and organize data for presentation. Thus, I would say that you want no more than three people working on this project.

Step 2: Don't Forget Hidden Time Stealers

Aside from the actual research time accumulated, you must add in the hidden time stealers, namely, management, writing, and production time.

MANAGEMENT

Management time is usually at least 10 percent of the research total. So, for the 165 hours tallied above, the project manager will probably spend at least 16 hours talking to the client, organizing staff, devising a research strategy, designing a questionnaire and, finally, presenting the report. That brings your running total to 182 hours.

I define management, for research purposes, as any activity other than actual research needed to complete the project. It is a critical job, one whose time requirements are often overlooked.

WRITING

Writing and analysis is another hidden factor. There are all kinds of writing required for a project. Writing up the results of an interview (which, by the way, should be done immediately following each phone call) is critical and can take twice as long as the interview itself. You can write your client memos or interim reports. Then there is the writing of the final report. My rule of thumb says you should expect two hours per report page. Those two hours include original writing time, rewriting, and proofing.

Writing may represent as much as 30 percent of the time you spend on the research itself, or in this case 50 hours (30 percent of 165 hours) project time.

PRODUCTION

Production, often considered the lowliest job, is the bottleneck that can make or break a project. It simply takes time to type or word-process the reports. Then, of course, producing charts or graphics—the aesthetics—can create all kinds of anxiety and soak up valuable time. These visual aids are essential, however, when dealing with such intangibles as information and intelligence. Allow time for their production.

In the example above, production represents 10 percent of the time spent on research, or 16 hours.

Step 3: Acknowledge the Fudge Factor

No matter how much planning you undertake, no matter how detailed your list of jobs and estimates of hours to be spent, you still must leave room for error. Remember that an estimate of how long a project will take is just that, an estimate.

During the course of research, many things can go wrong that may extend the project or push back the deadline. Your major contact is on vacation, a company's message system does not work, the entire company is at a meeting, your contact woke up on the wrong side of the bed this morning and hung up the phone on you, or—and this is the most nerve-wracking stumbling block—your research strategy was completely wrong and you have to start your project all over again.

For this eventuality, I recommend you add a fudge factor to all of your projects—no matter how many times you have completed similar projects, no matter how experienced you are.

Your fudge factor should represent a markup of at least 20 percent of your time. This is on top of all times estimated for management, writing, or production. By building a time cushion into your projects, you assure fewer frayed nerves and reasonable expectations on behalf of your staff.

Therefore, for the marketing strategy question I posed above, I recommend tacking on 50 hours (20 percent) onto the total of 258 hours. The total then is 308 hours, or seven and a half weeks for the entire project.

A Final Planning Note

I used the word *building* in this chapter title to describe an ongoing process. Even after you have assembled the appropriate staff, trained them, and established systems to undertake projects, you will still have to find ways to expand and improve the process. This will take time, patience, and foresight.

Special Issue: Should the Large Corporation Centralize Monitoring?

Virtually every large company I have investigated confronts the problem of how much they should centralize or decentralize competitor monitoring.

There are no easy answers here. Just be consoled that competitor monitoring is subject to the same whims and seesaw management battles as any other corporate function. Strategic planning and even accounting departments often shift location at many corporations, going from corporate to division and back again. Why should the competitor-monitoring function be immune from these shifts?

There a number of common-sense factors that will help you determine when and to what extent you want to decentralize your competitor-monitoring program. They are:

• *Company size.* Your company's size and geographic distribution are important factors to consider. For instance, a small company with only one location should maintain a central competitor-monitoring effort. However, if your organization is spread out all across the U.S. or the world, you will need a central headquarters office coordinating the effort, leaving the day-to-day intelligence gathering to the divisions.

• *Corporate structure.* Sometimes the way other corporate functions work within the context of your organization will dictate how you should structure competitor monitoring. For example, see how your company fits the strategic planning or marketing functions into your organization. Are these functions centralized, or are they scattered around the company? Is there a central office and a series of satellite offices located elsewhere in the company?

WHAT ROLE CAN CORPORATE PLAY?

Corporate headquarters, just like any division, will always need to do some of its own monitoring. But its most productive role is that of ringmaster, coordinator, and catalyst.

Here is how it can play that role best:

• *Become a central resource and switching station.* Headquarters should become a central networking resource for the rest of the company. It should be the place analysts and salespeople come to when they need to find an internal expert or to locate a esoteric market study in another division.

(continued)

MONITORING SNAPSHOT 25 (Continued)

- *Distribute Information.* Corporate should compile the complete competitive picture for the rest of the company, then distribute that information. A group of salespeople at Becton-Dickinson complained that too often they see only part of the picture. To remedy this problem, they have decided to get together at corporate, once a quarter, to pool information on a selected competitor. Corporate has agreed to act as the host for these conferences. Corporate has effectively become a clearinghouse for competitor information at Becton-Dickinson.

- *Facilitate brainstorming.* Corporate's job should be to identify and enlist the participation of experts throughout the company.

- *Create uniformity.* Corporate needs to insure that all divisions are using similar means of collecting, storing, and communicating information. It needs to create a template, a model that all divisions will follow. Such a template will help avoid duplication of research efforts and of resources.

CHAPTER 9

ETHICAL AND LEGAL GUIDELINES

Common sense, creativity, and just plain persistence—never bribery or theft—are the ingredients for a successful competitor-monitoring program. In my company and in most corporations, intelligence gatherers collect important data through a painstaking review of public documents and persistent interviewing. These researchers are successful without misrepresenting themselves, without trespassing, and without high-tech gadgetry.

Nevertheless, all intelligence gatherers face situations that tempt them to act illegally or unethically to collect information. To help you in those circumstances, this chapter gives a brief overview of the laws governing intelligence gathering, and discusses ways to develop ethical guidelines.

INTELLIGENCE GATHERING AND THE LAW

As in any business activity, stealing, trespassing, and bribery in the course of gathering intelligence are illegal. Some of the lesser-known legal pitfalls that you need to beware of are described below.

Antitrust Violation

Federal antitrust laws specifically prohibit companies from fixing prices or exchanging price information. The goal of the laws is to stop companies from conspiring to monopolize markets. While you are unlikely to violate the spirit of the law while gathering intelligence, you could violate the letter of the law if you swap information with a competitor. You should definitely consult your legal department before you ever discuss prices with a competitor, or even a competitor's representative, including distributors and wholesalers.

Also take note: Other countries outside the U.S. may not subject their corporations to the same antitrust restrictions. If you need to obtain intelligence on international competitors, your legal department should be consulted as to what your intelligence-gathering limits are, if any.

(For more information on antitrust laws and their impact on overall business activities, I recommend the *Anti-Trust Compliance Manual: A Guide for Counsel, Management, and Public Relations*, Walker B. Corngeys, Practising Law Institute, NY, April, 1986)

Discovering Intelligence Improperly

As long as you gather information generally considered in the public domain, you are unlikely to have legal problems. Once you start trying to find information that your competitors are protecting, then you enter risky territory. A case involving Du Pont highlights the subtle legal question of gathering intelligence improperly.

The Du Pont case was summarized by David Parker, a partner of the Manhattan law firm of Kraver & Parker, and the following passage was included in *Business Competitor Intelligence* (Wiley, 1984, page 299). The chapter was titled, "Legal Implications of Competitor Intelligence."

In 1969, Du Pont was in the middle of constructing a new methanol plant in Texas that made use of what Du Pont claimed was a highly secret but unpatented process. Du Pont claimed that the process was the result of expensive, time-consuming research that the company had taken special precautions to safeguard and that it gave Du Pont a competitive advantage over other producers. During the course of the construction, parts of the process (which would have eventually been enclosed within the plant) were exposed to view from the air.

Another party, presumably a competitor, hired photographers to take aerial pictures of the construction. Several pictures were taken and delivered to the presumed competitor. Du Pont, having seen the airplane circling over its plant and fearing that the photographs would enable a skilled person to deduce its secret process, contacted the photographers and asked them to reveal the name of the party who had hired them. When the photographers refused—citing their client's desire to remain anonymous—Du Pont sued the photographers.

Not surprisingly, one of the first things Du Pont did in the lawsuit was to demand as part of its pretrial discovery the identity of the photographer's client. The defendants again refused to make this disclosure and moved to dismiss the case. In essence, they said they had done nothing wrong: they had not trespassed, they had conducted their activities from public airspace, they had violated no government aviation standard, breached no confidential relationship, and engaged in no fraud or illegal conduct. Du Pont responded with a motion to compel the disclosure of the identity of the defendant photographers' client.

The district court denied the defendants' motion to dismiss and granted Du Pont's to compel. This decision was appealed to the United States Court of Appeals for the Fifth Circuit, which affirmed in an extended opinion.

The court of appeals further commented on what is considered "improper." The comment reads as follows:

> One may use his competitor's secret process if he discovers the process by reverse engineering applied to the finished product; one may use a competitor's process if he discovers it by his own independent research; but one may not avoid these labors by taking the process from the discoverer without his permission at a time when he is taking reasonable precautions to maintain its secrecy. To obtain knowledge of a process without spending the time and money to discover it independently is improper unless the holder voluntarily discloses it or fails to take reasonable precautions to ensure its secrecy.

Your legal department should review the subtle legal issues of intelligence gathering with you and develop a code of conduct for you. Most major corporations have such codes, although they are not well publicized.

INTELLIGENCE GATHERING AND ETHICS

Even if you comply with the letter of the law, you may encounter ethical dilemmas. Below is a case illustrating a potential ethical problem.

The Case: A Printer's Error

Version I: Clear-Cut

A marketing manager for a pharmaceutical company visited a printer to discuss the design of a new ad campaign. While in the waiting area, the marketing manager spotted a layout board revealing a competitor's marketing plans for the upcoming months. He immediately turned around and told his boss of the pricing strategy. His boss responded by changing his product's advertising strategy before the competitor's ads appeared. The competitor was stopped dead in its tracks.

Was the marketing manager wrong to use the information?

When I pose this case to my seminar audiences, almost everyone responds by saying the marketing manager did his duty. He reported information that he stumbled across. After all, he did not steal it. The information was literally under his nose.

Most in the audience will say that it was up to the printer to protect his client's property. Others state that the competitor should have insisted on the importance of maintaining absolute secrecy regarding the ad campaign.

But did the marketing manager commit a breach of ethics? Most will say no.

Version II: A Tinge of Gray

Now, what if we twist the story just slightly, as follows:

A marketing manager for a pharmaceutical company visited a printer to talk over the design of a new ad campaign. While in the waiting area, the marketing manager spotted a layout board for a competitor. The board was covered with thick, opaque tarpaulin. The marketing manager could not see through the cover. Yet there was a message on the tarpaulin. It read: "Confidential—Acme Pharmaceutical Company."

Should the marketing manager lift up the tarpaulin to obtain the information? Most executives who have heard this case at my seminars have responded no. When I ask them why, I first receive only silence. Then a few will state that they "feel funny going that far." They feel the advertisement is off limits and was meant to be that way.

Some in the audience say they have no problem lifting up the sheet. They are in the minority. Some half-jokingly will say they may just sidle up to the board and "accidentally" knock it over in the hope of uncovering it and learning what is underneath.

I call the difference in the two cases the Active/Passive Line. This is the line between passively finding information that the competitor has not protected and actively trying to obtain protected data. Crossing over this line is difficult and doing so causes a twinge in many people's hearts. Some equate such an action with the theft of a trade secret.

The situations that can challenge your ethical mettle are nearly endless. And since each of us has different values, I can't prescribe rules for how you should act. I can, though, offer you the following questions to ask yourself whenever you are confronted with an intelligence issue that brings you into the ethical gray areas.

1. Do I really need this information to make a sound decision? How much will this new information really help me or my company?

Too many executives gather competitor information out of fear that "something is over there, something that may cause me problems." Many managers ask for a level of detail they simply do not need to make a final business decision. Frankly, they may already have enough in hand to make that decision.

2. Have I exhausted all clearly ethical means?

You can sometimes run into a mental block, when you feel that you have followed every available avenue with no success. You may find yourself getting too emotionally involved in the case. Or a manager may be pressuring you for the information. When you reach that point, try to take a break. Remove yourself from the case temporarily. Forget about the specific information for a while until you can come back to it with a fresh mind.

Brainstorming with another colleague can also help you find alternative, ethical ways to locate competitor information.

3. What actions, in my gut, feel right or feel wrong?

This is the bottom-line question. If you, as that pharmaceutical executive, begin to imagine yourself spending a sleepless night after peeking at the price sheet under that tarpaulin, it's best not to look at it. In the long run, your self-respect is worth more than your job performance rating, no matter how severe the job pressures.

Remember also that unethical acts, once committed, pave the way for more unethical acts. Once you commit an act you consider unethical because you felt the pressure was too great, those same exceptions become easier and easier to make.

The Repercussions of Unethical Behavior

Much like a parent who is the role model for a child, a manager lays down the rules—both spoken and unspoken—that guide how his employees work and the rules they work by. If the information-gathering rules encourage unscrupulous behavior, you may have a hard time discouraging that behavior in other situations.

Unscrupulous behavior when gathering intelligence may lead to a general lowering of standards. It probably will also lower employees' opinion of your company, and make it easier for them to discard their loyalty for your firm. Why should any employee be loyal to a corporation that is unscrupulous?

Poor ethical conduct can be devastating to a company's morale, and potentially, to stockholder confidence in the company's management. It can also increase turnover, an expensive problem. So, conscience aside, unethical intelligence gathering can affect company health, wealth, and well-being—sooner or later.

THE 10 COMMANDMENTS OF INTELLIGENCE GATHERING

For your consideration, here are the 10 basic rules that guide my staff and me in our intelligence-gathering activities:

1. **Thou shalt not lie when representing thyself.**
   (For example: "I am but a poor, humble student writing a term paper.")

2. **Thou shalt observe thy company's legal guidelines as set forth by the legal department.**

3. **Thou shalt not tape-record a conversation.**

4. **Thou shalt not bribe.**

5. **Thou shalt not plant eavesdropping devices.**

6. **Thou shalt not deliberately mislead anyone in an interview.**

7. **Thou shalt neither obtain from nor give price information to thy competitor.**

8. **Thou shalt not swap misinformation.**

9. **Thou shalt not steal a trade secret (or steal employees away in hopes of learning a trade secret).**

10. **Thou shalt not knowingly press someone for information if it may jeopardize that person's job or reputation.**

SELECTED BOOKS ON BUSINESS ETHICS

I have not seen books that exclusively discuss the role of ethics in intelligence gathering, but I have found that general texts on business ethics address many of the ethical issues confronting intelligence gatherers.

I advise you to read at least one of them to give yourself and your colleagues a sense of where many of the gray areas exist and how far you may want to test the limits.

The following is a list of books written over the past 30 years on the subject of business ethics.

Bibliography

Above the Bottom Line: An Introduction to Business Ethics. Solomon, Robert C. New York: Harcourt, Brace, Jovanovich. 1983.

Bibliography of Business Ethics and Business Moral Values. Omaha, NB: College of Business Administration, Creighton Univ. 1984.

Business Ethics in America. Benson, George and Charles Sumner. Lexington, MA: Lexington Books. 1982.

Business Ethics: Concepts and Cases. Velasquez, Manuel G. Englewood Cliffs, NJ: Prentice-Hall. 1982.

Codes of Ethics in Corporations and the Teaching of Ethics in Graduate Business Schools. Opinion Research Corporation. Princeton, NJ: The Corporations. 1979.

Dollars and Sense of Honesty: Stories from the Business World. Armerding, George D. San Francisco, CA: Harper & Row. 1979.

Ethics for Executives Series. Harvard Business Review: 1955–1977.

Guides to Corporate Responsibility Series (Boston, 1958–1972). Harvard Business Review.

It's Good Business. Solomon, Robert C. New York: Atheneum. 1985.

Marketing Ethics: Guidelines for Managers Laczniak, Gene R., editor. Lexington, MA: Lexington Books. 1985.

Selected Bibliography of Applied Ethics in the Professions, 1950–70: A Working Sourcebook with Annotations and Indexes. Gothie, Daniel L. Charlottesville, VA: University Press of Virginia. 1973.

Tough Choices: Managers Talk Ethics. Barbara Toffler. New York: John Wiley & Sons, Inc. 1986.

CHAPTER 10

A CHECKLIST FOR COMPETITOR MONITORING

After reading this book, you should be able to assemble an effective competitor-monitoring program, but your busy schedule may not allow you the time to re-read this book as you develop your program. Therefore, I have designed a checklist to help stimulate your thinking and to help you address the major monitoring issues you must tackle.

IN THE BEGINNING

Have you done everything you can to track the competition without involving your organization? Have you begun to examine and use the following sources *regularly?*

- Commercial data bases
- Specialty trade publications
- Newsclippings

- Help-wanted advertisements
- Published studies
- Wall Street reports
- Trade-show and product literature
- Public filings
- Advertisements
- Personal contacts

Has your management officially backed the monitoring effort? Is there anyone among the senior managers who has agreed to act as champion, and who is willing to help you get money and personnel?

Have you found ways to involve the champion in the monitoring program? Does the champion recognize and offer thanks for outstanding intelligence contributions made by employees in the organization?

Have you set the correct intelligence-gathering goals? In other words, is the intelligence helping managers make critical decisions better or faster?

Have you drafted a brief mission statement, summarizing your competitor-monitoring goals? Have you publicized this statement to both the organization and to management?

RAISING AWARENESS

Does the organization generally understand senior management's intelligence needs? If not, why not? Have you communicated those needs?

Is your company aware of your intelligence effort? Have you tried . . .

- Sending out intelligence newsletters

- Posting notices on bulletin boards
- Speaking before special staff meetings
- Including competitor information in existing company newsletters

Do your colleagues fail to pass along intelligence because they are unaware of its importance, or because they don't want to bother? Have you investigated the reasons why intelligence isn't flowing to you?

PROVIDING INCENTIVES

Have you identified the departments that have competitor information but that may not want to relinquish that information? Have you offered them incentives such as those listed below?

- Swapping information
- Publishing their names or offering some kind of recognition
- Personal thanks from the champion for good information contributed by members of the group
- A cash reward for information

UNCOVERING HIDDEN INTELLIGENCE ASSETS

Have you identified departments, other than marketing or strategic planning, that may regularly collect a good deal of competitor information?

Some of these departments may include:

- Advertising
- Consulting
- Credit
- Customer service

- Distribution
- Government relations
- Legal
- Library
- Management information systems
- Meeting planning
- Personnel
- Production
- Public relations
- Purchasing
- Real estate
- Research & development
- Sales
- Strategic planning
- Training
- Treasury

Would your sales force find a hot line a useful tool for both giving and receiving intelligence?

Have you considered using your electronic mail system as a means of tapping into your company's hidden resources? Is your electronic mail system widely used and accepted as a communications tool?

Can you enforce the use of a competitor reporting form, or would it be considered another paperwork nuisance?

Is your organization so large and its pool of intelligence sources so deep that you need to consider conducting an intelligence audit? Have you identified a department which can provide you with fertile ground for testing the audit?

Have you identified volunteers to act as intelligence reps? If you have, are you providing the reps with adequate incentives, and are you using them judiciously?

ORGANIZING INTELLIGENCE

What kind of information do you need to organize? Statistics? Annual reports? Internal memos? The type of information often determines the way you store it.

Do you feel a centralized file will work best? Or should you keep the files decentralized in a place where those who need the files, such as salespeople, can have easy access to it?

Have you created an index for your files? Have you distributed this index to the files' primary users?

Have you designed the files to meet the users' needs? For example, if company engineers use the files, you may want to consider collecting patent filings.

Have you included the following items in your files?
- Annual reports
- Securities and Exchange Commission reports, or other government filings
- News articles
- Product literature
- Price lists
- Market studies
- Business-school cases

- General public filings
- Internal memos
- Strategic plans
- Sales-call reports
- Hot-line inquiries
- Competitor reports
- Product evaluations

Have you carefully considered how the following types of data bases can help your monitoring program?

- Spreadsheet
- Directory
- Textual

If you are thinking about a mainframe-based system, do you have the large budget necessary to support such a system?

Are you sure the way you have designed the data entry process so that the system can end up delivering the information in a timely manner?

Will the data base offer any value added?

Before going headlong into a new system, have you checked to see if others in your organization have already created similar data bases that contain competitor information?

Have you organized the data base simply and appropriately? Can the information be organized in a manner even simpler than your current format?

Are you entering too much information? Would it be best for some of the information to remain on paper?

Have you established goals for your data base? Make sure your data base is reaching the right audience and meeting their needs; otherwise, you could be wasting their time—and yours!

THE LIBRARY AS A RESOURCE

Have you designed your intelligence library as a directory, rather than a repository? Remember, you cannot afford, nor do you need, to build a Library of Congress.

Have you collected the best and most appropriate sources for your library? These would include:

- General reference books
- Periodical indexes
- Industry-specific sources

Are you using the library's monitoring services to the fullest? Are you and your intelligence users aware of the full array of library services?

DELIVERING INTELLIGENCE

Are you using the following tools to communicate intelligence to the general organization?

- Newsletters
- Displays
- Electronic mail

Are you using the following tools to communicate intelligence to key decision makers?

- Reports

- Reference books
- Newsclippings

BUILDING AN INTELLIGENCE DEPARTMENT

Are you hiring the right analysts for your needs?

Are you using all available options to find analysts?

Do the analysts you hire have the following traits and skills?

- Creativity
- Desire
- Interviewing skills
- Writing skills

Do you concentrate analyst training on the following areas?

- Knowledge of secondary sources
- Data-base training
- Writing
- Telephone interviewing
- Financial analysis
- Technical training
- Sales
- Spreadsheet packages

Do you usually give the new analyst some test assignments through which he can learn the various skills and gain certain knowledge of the research process?

Have you devised ways to control research costs? Have you tried the following?

- Delegating the intelligence gathering to others outside the research staff
- Charging back services
- Using timesheets to track dollars and time spent

Do your project managers know how to take proper research requests?

Is project time being planned for properly? Is a fudge factor being built into projects?

LEGALITIES AND ETHICS

Have you drawn up a legal and ethical guide for your competitor-monitoring program?

Have you examined the antitrust laws you must watch out for?

Are all of your intelligence reps or analysts collecting information carefully and within the prescribed guidelines?

Are you or your staff misrepresenting yourselves in any way when conducting interviews?

Are you compromising someone else's job or livelihood because of your activity?

Is the research staff aware of the difference between a trade secret and a patent and how that may affect the information you collect and how you collect it?

Have you discussed ethics and legality with your staff, especially with regard to intelligence gathering? Are ethics given lip service and no more?

SURVEY OF CORPORATE INTELLIGENCE GATHERING

INTRODUCTION AND METHODOLOGY—1985 SURVEY SUMMARY

In July and August 1985, Information Data Search conducted in-depth interviews with managers in charge of gathering corporate intelligence for 25 Fortune-500 companies. In August 1986, Information Data Search surveyed managers at 50 more companies, many of which were smaller than Fortune-500 firms. The 1986 results confirmed the 1985 findings. The report below is a summary of the 1985 findings.

The study focused on two questions: First, how do large corporations in various industries collect competitor intelligence and then disseminate that information to key decision makers? Second, what systems and organizational structures characterize successful intelligence departments?

Interviews were conducted with executives in all 25 corporations and

---

Conducted by Information Data Search, Inc.

visits were made to 8 of these companies. Interviews were also conducted with two data-base/software suppliers who design products for use in intelligence gathering.

The companies surveyed are in the following industries:

- Appliances
- Banking
- Chemicals
- Communications
- Electronics
- Financial services
- Food processing
- Publishing

EXECUTIVE SUMMARY

- All the companies surveyed have an individual, a group within a department, or a full department devoted to gathering competitor intelligence. Although the intelligence gatherers in many companies have other duties as well, every company has at least the equivalent of one full-time employee gathering competitor information.

- All the companies surveyed have increased their intelligence-gathering budgets substantially in the past five years. In fact, approximately one-third of the companies surveyed did not even have a separate intelligence-gathering function or department five years ago.

- The companies surveyed spend an average of $450,000 annually to track their competition.

- Many of the most successful intelligence departments have not built—nor do they intend to build—data bases to track the competition. Instead, they rely solely on manual filing systems and an active network of internal experts for their business intelligence.

- The companies that have used computer data bases most successfully for competitor intelligence have kept the data bases small and simple. The successful data bases generally are maintained on micro-computers, rather than minicomputers or mainframes.

• Many large-scale competitor data bases, especially those on main-frames, have fallen into disuse. Major reasons for data-base failure include:

> • *Maintenance expense often overlooked by data-base designers*
> • *Difficulties in keeping information current*
> • *Poor communication to the rest of the company about the benefits of the data base*
> • *Lack of priorities on information to be input*

• To be successful, a new intelligence department very much needs a champion within senior management to fight for an appropriate budget and to help the department gain the cooperation of other important divisions in the company.

• Many intelligence managers believe that it takes three to five years for an intelligence department to become truly effective. In that time the department must win the trust of other departments and develop a network of contacts within the company. The department must also train staff members in the various skills needed to gather intelligence effectively and efficiently.

• The most effective intelligence departments undertake awareness campaigns to persuade others in the organization of the value of competitor information. The awareness campaign also makes known the availability of such information.

• Sales departments often contain the most valuable competitor information and are often the least cooperative in relinquishing it.

• The most effective intelligence departments find they earn much more support when they anticipate management's intelligence needs, rather than continually reacting to "ad hoc" requests for information. Staff limitations, however, make it difficult for many departments to fulfill even the ad hoc requests.

DETAILS OF FINDINGS

1. INTELLIGENCE DEPARTMENT AGES

Highlights

• The average age of all the intelligence-gathering departments surveyed is 7.7 years.

• Companies in mature industries such as food processing or chemicals are more likely to have older, well-established intelligence departments. Conversely, companies in newer or more dynamic industries have younger intelligence departments.

• The intelligence departments in three well-established, $1 billion-plus companies are over 20 years old.

• In most cases, those companies operating in the banking or telecommunications industries have intelligence-gathering departments that are less than five years old.

• The newest department, in a relatively young company, is less than three months old.

Findings from Intelligence Leaders

• The departments that appear to be the most effective information gatherers are at least five years old, or have executives running them who have been at the company for five or more years.

2. INTELLIGENCE DEPARTMENT ORIGINS

Highlights

• Most companies established the intelligence function (i.e., assigned someone to gather intelligence) to meet a specific, short-term need. Only a few companies in the survey established an intelligence-gathering function as part of a long-term plan.

• The permanent position of "intelligence analyst" often evolved because one person demonstrated a "knack" for this type of research. In a few instances, the appointment to the position of "intelligence analyst" resulted from a specific request by a senior manager.

• In most companies surveyed, intelligence gathering is not yet a separate department. In the companies in which intelligence gathering is a separate department, the intelligence-gathering function evolved into a department only when a key decision maker thought it necessary. The change from "function" to "department" usually came about by executive edict.

• In a few instances, the department or function was created in reaction to a specific event or change in the marketplace—such as deregulation.

Findings from Intelligence Leaders

• The companies that are most successful at intelligence gathering usually established an intelligence-gathering position or department as part of a long-term planning process.

3. INTELLIGENCE DEPARTMENT BUDGETS

Highlights

• Intelligence-gathering budgets range from less than $50,000 to over $1.5 million for a single department. The average annual budget for the companies surveyed is $450,000.

• Almost one-third of the respondents reported budgets of at least $1 million. Only two respondents reported budgets of less than $50,000.

• Professional salaries represent an average of 47 percent of the intelligence budget for these departments.

• Support salaries represent an average of 12 percent of the intelligence budget.

• Materials and equipment purchases represent an average of 16 percent of the intelligence budget.

• Contract research (that is, vendors hired by the company to conduct research) represents an average of 16 percent of the intelligence budget.

• Training receives the smallest average expenditure, representing approximately 3 percent of the budget.

Findings from Intelligence Leaders

• Intelligence leaders generally have larger intelligence-gathering budgets; however, several firms with large budgets were not among the most effective intelligence operations.

• The intelligence leaders spend a much higher percentage of their budgets on professional staff than do the other intelligence departments.

• On average, most leaders also spend a much higher percentage on contract research.

4. THE INTELLIGENCE DEPARTMENT'S POSITION WITHIN THE ORGANIZATION

Highlights

• Less than one-third of the companies surveyed maintain separate intelligence-gathering departments. Instead, intelligence gathering is generally the responsibility of from one to four people within the marketing, market research, or corporate-planning departments.

• The library or information center is often part of the intelligence-gathering "group" but is not usually exclusively assigned to gather competitor intelligence. All but one of the twenty-five companies surveyed have a corporate library that performs general information collection for corporate intelligence purposes.

• On average, the intelligence-gathering function is two levels removed from the decision maker in the organization.

Findings from Intelligence Leaders

• Those intelligence-gathering departments with the most timely market information are often located in divisions, not at the corporate level.

• Successful corporate-based intelligence groups have a well-established network of contacts and intelligence-gathering representatives at the divisional level. They can thus tap information that many corporate level departments ignore.

5. ORGANIZATION CHARTS

The following selection of organization charts displays the wide variety of structures that accommodate an intelligence-gathering function.

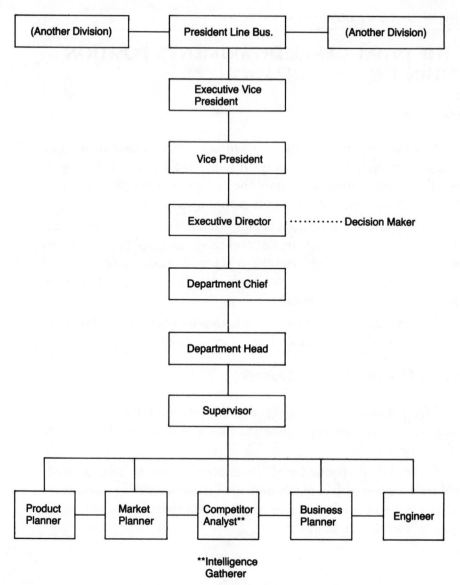

Figure A-1 Organization Chart for $1 billion plus electronics company

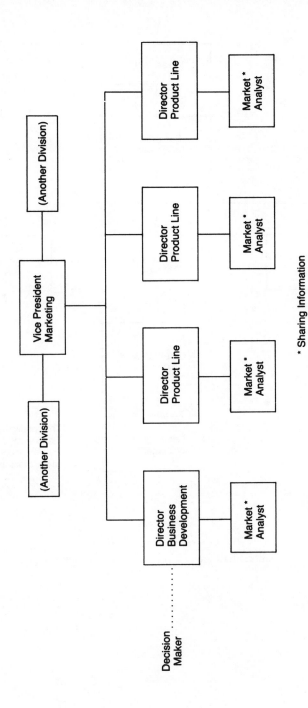

Figure A-2 Organization Chart for $500 million plus computer hardware company

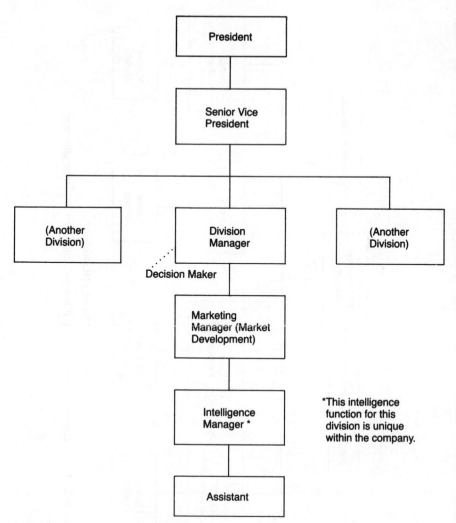

Figure A-3 Organization chart for $10 billion consumer packaged goods company

6. SOURCES USED

Highlights

• Over 50 percent of the respondents rely almost exclusively on published sources for information. These sources include magazine and newspaper articles, data bases, and annual reports.

• Fewer than 30 percent of the respondents extensively used primary sources such as interviews or internal reports (e.g., sales-call reports) to systematically track the competition.

• Independently published marketing reports are rarely used by respondents to update their files.

Findings from Intelligence Leaders

• The successful departments take a more active stance when updating their files. They conduct more interviews and use internal reports far more often than do the other firms.

Analysis and Comments

• Many of the respondents were surprised when asked how often they used internal reports and correspondence. Many had not even considered using this resource.

• Interviews and interview transcripts are almost never incorporated into competitor files. This may be because conducting original interviews is too time-consuming for small staffs.

7. INTERNAL INFORMATION SOURCES

Highlights

• Marketing and sales were cited most often as the best internal sources for competitor information.

• Sales was also cited as the department least offering to share competitive information.

• Although various departments, such as sales, are often uncooperative, respondents believe that there are ways to open up the channels of communication between the intelligence group and other departments.

Findings from Intelligence Leaders

• While the intelligence leaders also experience resistance from various groups within their companies, they seem to experience less of it. The reason for their relative success seems to be longevity. Intelligence leaders have had more time to build an internal network.

• The leaders have almost uniformly established "intelligence committees" to tap information available on a divisional level. This is especially crucial when the intelligence department is located at the corporate level.

Analysis and Comments

• Lack of cooperation, not small budgets, appears to be the major stumbling block in many companies' attempts to build internal intelligence systems. Without the cooperation of departments like sales, a company is losing some of its best sources for industry intelligence.

• Various respondents agreed that the intelligence department can take several steps to make other departments more cooperative. For instance, if the intelligence department can produce useful information for the other departments, these departments will see that cooperation may be in their self-interest. In addition, the intelligence department might try to convince management to implement a compensation program for those employees providing competitor information.

8. COMPUTERIZED DATA BASES

Highlights

• Over half of the companies interviewed maintain a computerized data base containing information about various competitors.

• In most cases, maintenance costs run at least as high or higher than the data base's start-up costs.

• Over half the companies spent in excess of $100,000 to build their competitor data base. (This figure includes all salaries and equipment applied to constructing a system.)

• The average annual data base maintenance cost has been approximately $172,500.

• Approximately 50 percent of those with computerized data bases operate them on microcomputers.

• Operating costs have been far higher for data bases maintained on a mainframe system than for microcomputer-based systems.

• In many instances companies have instituted data bases that later fell into disuse. Companies abandoned data bases for some of the following reasons:
   • They were difficult, complex, and expensive to update.
   • They duplicated information that was available elsewhere—either on other data bases or in printed form (e.g., an annual report).
   • They did not meet the specific needs of the decision makers.
   • Users were never educated about the specific benefits provided by the data base.

• Several companies are re-examining the efficacy of competitor data bases. Those intelligence departments with limited budgets are often shifting dollars and staff time away from data bases and into improving their relationships with other departments in the company.

• A few companies with large intelligence budgets have chosen to maintain large data bases, but even these companies have shifted some resources toward internal networking and staff training.

Findings from Intelligence Leaders

• Intelligence leaders do not necessarily use data bases. One of those leaders interviewed does not even maintain a data base. Another maintains small microcomputer data bases scattered throughout the company.

• Of those that are constructing or have constructed large data bases on mainframes, all received approval from either a senior vice-president or from the president or chief executive officer of the corporation.

Analysis

• There appear to be two generations of competitor data bases in the corporate world. The first generation was launched from the mid-seventies to the early eighties. They were developed before the microcomputer was readily accepted in corporate offices, and thus often shared large computers with other data bases and programs. Many of these systems evolved with little forethought as to who their users were or what purpose the data base was to serve. Based on the reports of the companies interviewed, these data bases rarely appear to be worth the expense and staff time they require.

• The second generation competitor data bases were designed approximately two years ago, after price drops for microcomputers and the increasing availability of sophisticated microcomputer software. Microcomputer data bases are much cheaper and usually easier to access and update than mainframe data bases. They have generally proved more successful, although some companies did note that these data bases have not lived up to expectations.

(Please note: Because of the proliferation of the microcomputer within corporations, the particular data base discussed by a respondent may be one of many that exist within his or her company. That being the case, we asked each respondent to discuss the one with which he or she is most familiar.)

9. INDEXED FILES

Highlights

• Over half the respondents have more than 20 file cabinets within 50 feet of their offices.

• Most respondents stated that there is no index for any of these files.

• In most instances where the files are indexed, the cabinets belong to the library and are cross-referenced with the card catalog.

Findings from Intelligence Leaders

• Many of the intelligence leaders already have their file cabinets indexed. The index can be found in either a card catalog or on a computerized data base.

Analysis and Comments

• Indexes are far easier to construct than a full-fledged data base. Many companies have realized this and have built an online index for their entire file cabinet system. These indexes allow easy access to information already available within the organization.

10. COMMUNICATING INFORMATION TO MANAGEMENT

Highlights

• The number of competitor memos or reports issued by the intelligence groups surveyed ranges from one report every six months to twelve per week.

• Based on samples submitted, these reports can vary widely in size and scope. The shortest memo may have a few sentences and a news-clipping attached. The longest may be a comprehensive competitive analysis.

Findings from Intelligence Leaders

• The most effective intelligence gatherers issue frequent reports and memoranda. These communications keep intelligence departments in touch with their constituency, and help the intelligence gatherers get better cooperation in their searches for information.

• Intelligence leaders appear to have very open-ended reporting periods, or none at all. The leaders send memos when the information merits it, not just at month-end or year-end.

• One intelligence leader prefers not to issue memos at all. Because of the fast-changing nature of his business, he responds by telephone or direct meeting. Again, he has no fixed reporting period and prefers not to be hampered by such a structure.

Analysis and Comments

• The rule of thumb seems to be that the more frequent the intelligence memo, the fresher the intelligence, and the more the information is listened to and acted on.

11. GAINING MANAGEMENT'S ATTENTION

Highlights

• Most respondents believe that memos or meetings will encourage senior management to pay attention and act on a vital piece of information.

• Some intelligence managers have established companywide committees to discuss competitive issues. These meetings are forums for disseminating information collected by the intelligence department, as well as for making initial strategic decisions.

• In three instances, the intelligence managers stated that they did not have to "get management's attention," because senior management was itself aggressively looking for competitor information. In these cases, management is seeking out the intelligence department.

Findings from Intelligence Leaders

• The leaders have close ties with senior management and have little problem gaining their attention.

• Some of the most effective intelligence departments have their offices close to those of senior management. Managers thus often wander into the intelligence department and can easily keep abreast of important information.

Analysis and Comments

• Interviewees cited a number of strategies they have used to convince management to act on competitor information. The following are some quotes:

• "We have formed a Central Planning Review Committee to meet once a month."

• "I have held 7 a.m. meetings with the CEO. His workday has just started and he does not feel extremely pressured early in the morning. Because his meeting calendar does not begin until 8:30 or so, he has many times extended our meetings—which could not be done any other time in the day."

• "I have found that a casual discussion is sometimes the best means to get a senior manager to listen to you. I can recall a number of instances where a senior VP has come down to our product demo room to see what a competitor's product actually looks like and to ask technical questions of our engineers, directly. Because a senior VP will not hesitate to come down to our shop, we can keep him informed on the latest issues and manage to cut through any rumors he may have heard along the way."

12. BENEFITS PROVIDED BY INTELLIGENCE-GATHERING DEPARTMENTS

Highlights

• A number of respondents stated that, because of their intelligence-gathering efforts, they were able to warn management of a competitor's impending move. Management was then able to take immediate action that reduced the potential damage.

• Many respondents found it difficult to name specific instances in which the competitor or industry information they provided measurably affected the fortunes of the company. They believe, however, that the information they gather generally enables management to make better strategic decisions.

Findings from Intelligence Leaders

• Intelligence leaders were more likely to give detailed accounts of their successes. One manager, for example, described how his advance knowledge of a competitor's new-product release allowed his firm to flood the market with price-cutting coupons. This action allowed his firm to maintain a strong foothold in the market, and at the same time hindered his competitor's chances to launch its new product successfully.

13. MAJOR PROBLEMS FACING INTELLIGENCE DEPARTMENTS

Highlights

• Almost half the managers surveyed stated that they have significant problems keeping their competitor file folders or data bases current.

• Many respondents find it difficult to educate their peers in other functional areas about the availability and usefulness of competitor information.

• Respondents generally believe that they are unable to locate all the relevant intelligence already available somewhere within their corporation. Reasons cited for this problem include: lack of a central filing system; no organized comprehensive routing list; and geographical and political obstacles.

Findings from Intelligence Leaders

• Even those respondents who appeared fairly successful in collecting and disseminating competitor data believe they are missing a good deal of valuable information located within their organization.

1986 SURVEY SUMMARY

The 1986 survey generally confirmed the findings of the 1985 study, and indicated that smaller companies are also devoting increasing resources to competitor intelligence. Below is a summary of the 1986 findings.

METHODOLOGY

• Telephone interviews were conducted with executives in over 50 companies.

• While the 1985 survey focused on Fortune-500 companies, the 1986 survey included firms with sales less than $100 million. One half of the 1986 sample included Fortune-500 companies.

• About half of the 1986 sample consisted of service firms; the 1985 sample was only about one-quarter service firms.

Highlights

• Over 82 percent of respondents reported intelligence budgets of less than $200,000.

• Smaller firms generally reported smaller budgets, which explains why the 1985 average ($450,000) was much higher.

• As in 1985, almost all firms reported significant growth in intelligence spending in the last five years, and most firms expected that growth to continue.

• Almost 25 percent of respondents reported that they had no intelligence budget five years ago; these firms now have intelligence budgets averaging approximately $50,000 annually.

• Despite the increase in funding for competitor intelligence, no respondent worked for a department that solely gathered intelligence. Most respondents worked for marketing or corporate planning.

• 50 percent of the respondents felt that lack of funding and staff prevented them from effectively monitoring the competition.

• Aside from budgets, most respondents felt that organizational problems within their companies were the biggest roadblocks to gathering data. Respondents cited lack of awareness as the single biggest organizational problem they faced. Respondents in general believed that organizational issues were much more important than lack of computer power.

• As in the 1985 sample, less than half of the respondents used computerized data bases to track the competition. Of the computer users, only one-third used a mainframe. The rest generally used microcomputer-based spreadsheets and data base packages.

• While budget size appeared to have some impact on the success of the intelligence systems, it did not appear to be the sole factor. Several well-organized, low-budget programs appeared to be as effective in gathering and communicating information as were programs several times bigger.

INDEX

About the author

Leonard M. Fuld is President and founder of Information Data Search, Inc., a Cambridge, Massachusetts-based firm that specializes in gathering "competitor intelligence." His company has been featured on the "Today" show, CBS Network "Newsbreak," in the *Harvard Business Review, Venture Magazine,* and *Marketing News.* He is the author of *Competitor Intelligence: How to Get It—How to Use It* (Wiley, 1985), and has contributed to *Business Competitor Intelligence* (Wiley, 1984). In addition, Mr. Fuld is the editor of a quarterly newsletter on corporate intelligence gathering, called *Intelligence Update.*